# Twenty First Century Prophets

# 21st Century Prophets
Bishop Rodney S. Walker, I

Published by Bishop R.S. Walker Ministries formerly Another
Touch of Glory Press
2760 Crain Highway
Waldorf, Maryland 20601
Voice (301-843-9267) - (877-200-8967)
Fax (240-585-7093)
Web address: http://www.bishoprswalker.com
E-mail: admin@bishoprswalker.com

ISBN-13: 978-0692434659 (Bishop R S Walker Ministries)
ISBN-10: 0692434658

# Acknowledgements
Recognition of Contributions

I would like to take this opportunity to thank and acknowledge **Dr. Amanda F. Standard** Founder & Artistic Director of Divine Dance Institute (DDI) for your support and assistance in the preparation of this book for publication. I appreciate your willingness to meet the challenges of teaching and sharing such an important subject as Prophetic Dance.

Thanks to **Psalmist Cassandra Ross** for your support and assistance teaching the role of the Prophetic Psalmist in the body of Christ and in the Prophetic. Your private and public life clearly indicates your intimate relationship with God. We appreciate and celebrate your giftedness in your ministry.

**Thank You...** To my son, Rodrick Walker, for your contribution in developing the Book Cover. To Elder Valerie Rogers, for your contribution with formatting and organizing. To Elder Moira Washington and Elder-Elect Carla Aultmon, for your contributions with editing. To Elder Kelly Putman, Carlyn Walker and Elder Cynthia V. White for your support and assistance in preparing the book for publication. I appreciate your willingness to meet the challenges necessary to prepare this product for printing and distribution. Thank you to all of my students at Another Touch of Glory School of the Prophets for the great questions and demand you cultivate which assist in developing me as a Prophet. Your ideas and suggestions contributed immensely to the success of this project. It is good to have all of you as part of the team. I am confident that good things will come from our joint efforts. There is no way I could get this project completed by my efforts alone. Thank you, again, for a job well done.

# Dedication

This book is dedicated to my lovely wife Pastor Betty A. Walker. She has been an extraordinary blessing to me and provides tremendous support with all of my writing projects. Her encouragement and assistance, in every area of preparation, is greatly appreciated. Thank your Betty! I could not do this without you.

# Introduction

This is an exciting and necessary time we are living in, particularly as Prophets and Apostles in the body of Christ. Being a 21$^{st}$ Century Prophet is more than prophesying and telling someone what God is saying they will get in the next few days. Our job as Prophets has gone much further than that. We have great responsibilities - like making sure that people in the body of Christ are staying on course in what God is saying they are to do and become. Prophets in this season are to deal with governmental things that keep the body on point with things that are to manifest in difficult times like these. Many of us in the body of Christ have no idea what is required in this day and it is time for prophetic people and prophets that walk in the office of the Prophet. This is the reason I write books like the 21st Century Prophet.

The Prophet in this season looks different. In times past the Prophet had to deal with things in a demonstrative way. In these times, God is pushing us to experience things so we could pray and speak from a place of someone else's experience. In this season God may have a Prophet to spiritually or physically experience what some have dealt with so that they could pray differently.

Along with being able to pray different, 21st Century Prophets may also take on a different look. They function like a prophet, but take on the look of an executive, a president of a company, a singer or may even look like a stay at home mom. They are no longer those that wear the prophetic garbs as Elijah, but rather a suit without a ministry title.

The 21st Century Prophet is more concerned with the assignment than with their appearance as a prophet. Clothes do not make the Prophet more than the Prophet being made by characteristics, gifting, signs and wonders. There are certain giftings that frequent the Prophet's life. But because we are in the 21st century, the Prophet must take on a different look in order get in different kind of doors.

We miss so many opportunities to make a difference in our lifetime because we don't know who we are and how to properly administer the gifts that God has given us to improve, change and/or reverse demonic influence in the lives of the people of God and all of God's creation.

The opportunity in the Old Testament for Elijah was to change the financial status of a widow woman. Well, that assignment did not change just because we came into a different time. The only thing that changed about that was who needed the change and the person that brought that change. Elijah brought financial healing to the woman by asking her, "what do you have in the house" and the 21st Century Prophet asked you, "What talent or gifting do you have that could be turned into a profit center for you?" What did they both do? They both evaluated what the person had to work with. As a 21st Century Prophet, you have to evaluate where a person is or may be at the time. The evaluation may be mentally, financially or emotionally.

There are eight exciting chapters in this book that will lead you to a greater understanding of the Office and functioning of the Prophet. One topic covered in this book is "The Prophet's Mantle (The Gift of Access)". What is the mantle? How is it used? If you are a Prophet, you need to know the keys that unlock the mantle of the Prophet; and in this book you will discover these keys and how to apply them in the 21st Century. We find that everything in the Old Testament, New Testament and in biblical times is still in force. We just need to know how to apply them in the 21st Century.

You will discover how to differentiate a Prophet from an Intercessor in the traditional sense, and how to distinguish the difference between prophetic intercession and priestly intercession. Prophets are the mouth piece of God, therefore the operation of this gift in people who are called to the "Office of the Prophet" is very different than many people have imagined. There are certain keys that unlock the mantle of the prophet and in this book you will learn these keys.

How is prophetic evangelism different from traditional evangelism and how can it be applied in the market place? We talk about that and this will be a tremendous blessing for you if you understand and practice Prophetic Evangelism. What does prophetic deliverance look like in the 21st Century? You will be amazed to find out that you can actually minister deliverance prophetically. As you think about this, you have to understand that God has a desire to minister deliverance to people, churches, businesses, etc. It is the prophet's job to bring that kind of liberation. As a Prophet, churches, businesses, or even families may call for you; but because people don't understand the assignment of 21st Century Prophets, they will criticize your assignment it. Some people have spiritual problems in their churches and don't know how to solve them. The Prophet is to know exactly how to solve the problem.

The Prophet's job is to come in with strategies and plans to eliminate problems. I can remember this one church called our prophetic team in but when it was time to function in the strategy, they did not desire to do it. Their church continued with the problem until it went down. I can remember people that would say, "I suffer with this problem with homosexuality and I need deliverance. Can you help me?" I answered, "Yes I can, but you have to do exactly what I tell you to do. If you fail to obey, you would have to start all over again. Do you understand?" They answered, "Yes." I proceeded to tell them, "somewhere along the line you left a door open and even if this happened to you before you could do anything about it, you kept allowing it in the days when you could have stopped

it. Now you have to make a big decision to shut it down."
They obeyed and shut it down. 2 Chronicles 20:20
"**...Believe in the Lord your God, so shall ye be
established; believe His prophets, so shall ye prosper**."
You will also learn how important it is to use faith in the realm
of prophetic ministry. There are concepts that you must know
and follow in order to get the expected results and actually
walk in the fullness of the blessings of God. What is prophetic
praise and worship? How important is the role of the Psalmist
in our worship experience? How do you take dominion over
the kingdoms of this world prophetically? These answers are
all in this book and many more.

# Table of Contents

# Contents

# Chapter 1

## The Prophets Mantle (The Gift of Access)

There are certain principles that unlock the mantle of the Prophet and in this class you will learn twelve of those keys that we have never released in any class. This new class material every Prophet must learn or continue to walk in. There are three principles that cause the release of power and we will talk about them in this session.

*We must understand that there are various mantles in various areas of leadership. If one desired the mantle of their leader, they had to understand and learn to walk in the three principles for functioning that causes a release on them of the same power, grace and anointing that rests on your leader/Father.*

*Wearing the mantle is common for the person that serves as the Successor of the leader/Father. It would not be incorrect to call this the "Mantle of Succession". The Successor knows how to effectively handle the leader's mantle just as they learned how to handle their leader. If you don't know how to handle the leader, you will not know how to handle his mantle. Let's look at the three principles:*

**Principle # 1** *Succession: You can be a Successor like Joshua and Elisha were and receive the mantle of your leader or you can follow the example of Gehazi, Elisha's servant who failed to receive the mantle due to greed operating in his heart. The principle of succession is simple: as you walk under the hand of your leader and serve well, his mantle comes on you. We find that Elisha served well and got double of what was on his leader. By his example, we will see that there are some things he did that stands out:*

1. *He refused to listen to other voices around him.*
2. *He served closer than anyone else around him.*
3. *He served without quitting and was given reason to do so by Elijah.*
4. *He created an unwavering focus on purpose.*
5. *He stayed in proper and Prophetic alignment with his leader.*

**Principle # 2** *Serving Well: Every leader that serves well captures the spirit of his leader. Many people will never receive their leader's spirit because they fail at the serving level. Serving opens up your leader's heart towards you when ordinarily his heart would not have opened. Why not? You must realize that your leader sees and serves many people yet feels all alone when it is time to accomplish the assignment or when he is pouring out and there is no evidence those following him are receiving. When your heart opens to help him his heart does likewise in releasing to you.*

*Principle # 3: Submission:* *Submission is defined as (1) a willingness to yield or surrender to somebody, the act of doing so or (2) demanding nothing less than total submission to someone in authority.*

### What Is A Mantle?

**A Mantle** is a loose-fitting garment worn by Prophets and other officials in authority to signify their position and power to exercise dominion. Mantles reflect latitude, stature, prestige, and provisions of the wearer, as well as the license to act.

We must understand how a mantle operates for a Prophet for the power and authority of a Prophet lies in the mantle. The mantle is designed to keep you going, providing protection in the most adverse conditions. Just as Elisha upon receiving the mantle used it to cross back over the Jordan River, the mantle is designed to cause break-through for you when used properly. Had he not carefully observed Elijah create a crossing point of dry land in the midst of the Jordan, Elisha would not have known how to use the mantle to get back over the Jordan. His ability to strike the river with the mantle to cross it resulted from him purposing to remain close to his leader and to observe what he did. Otherwise Elisha would have been stuck on the wrong side of the river and would not have been delivered.

*As a successor you have to have the same heart for the assignment your leader has. If your leader has a heart for intercession, you have to embrace that as well. If your leader has a heart for the prophetic, you have to embrace that as well. Often times you have to be the runner or the mediator, the one who serves as the go between.*

**Therefore turn thou to thy God: keep mercy and judgment, and wait on thy God continually.**
*Hosea 12:6*

As we look at the setting of this verse in **Hosea 12:1-6**, we find both the Nation of Judah and the Nation of Israel in a backslidden condition and God calling the people back to repentance and fellowship with Him. We can use, as an example, Jacob who struggled with God to make it back to a place of favor in Him. It is important to see who God called to this place of intercession for the people. God calls for the Prophet to intercede for and speak prophetically to the people. God would also call for the Prophet to prophesy the people into destiny, and before doing so, the Seer/Intercessor comes to break up fallow ground. It must be understood that the Intercessor at this time may be called to the Prophet's side. They both will come to melt the hearts of the hardhearted and also to clear the atmosphere of hindrances. This kind of word is easily received once the Seer/Intercessor has done their job. God is saying return! Now, understanding that the Prophet is on assignment and so is the Intercessor, the thing we should see is that the mantle of the Prophet could come on the intercessor or successor at this time of serving the Prophet. Both the intercessor and successor that serves the Prophet must know how to treat the vestments of the Prophet.

**Mantle Treatment** is defined as that which is learned, practiced, supplied to, and provided for within the mantle of ministers in order to equip and empower them for service to the Lord. These treatments are beyond normal church attendance and believer's Bible studies. Mentoring, schools of ministry (especially for the Prophet and the Apostle), and ministry apprenticeship are needed for effective treatment of one's mantle. These preparations are usually above what the typical Christian receives or is exposed to in church services. Their distinction is that these treatments help ministers serve more competently and confidently in the execution of their assigned posts.

### *Keep mercy and judgment*

Mercy is the place of mediation; a place of intercession; and where we prefer others above ourselves. This is where principle #3 is enforced. The successor at this point is not going according to what he thinks but according to what the Prophet knows. Although neither of them is mercy driven, God powerfully moves through them in Prophetic intercession, revealing the mind and purpose of God to them. Remember, the Prophet is doing what is in the mind of God and the successor is doing what is in the mind of the Prophet. While the Prophet intercedes and is being sensitized to what God desire to happen, they are under strict orders not to speak, but to pray as an Intercessor. It is at this time of sensitivity and intimacy that the successor gets into the heart of the Prophet. Remember the word "assignment". As the Prophet shifts into his assignment, the assignment of the successor shifts and he comes closer to the mantle.

*Let us therefore come boldly unto the throne of grace, that we may obtain mercy and find grace to help in time of need.*     *Hebrew 4:16*

*So here we come into intercession with a real sense of dying to who we are, and to who we think we are, as we become aware of our place of intercession or the place of assignment. In a counseling session, you don't look to say much for yourself. Look at this as **inter – session**. You enter a session to make something happen for someone else. We violate the whole principle of succession when we don't learn to enter a session on someone else's behalf. This is a learned art that is a powerful principle of succession. We are using intercession as an example but I think you are really getting it. This is going to teach you how to embrace the heart of your leader.*

**Place of judgment**
Judgment is truth, coming back to a place of divine order, keeping His counsel, and obedience to His laws. The place of judgment is the place of "prophetic influence". The very heart of the Father is mercy and the very heart of the Prophet is results. When we understand the heart of the leader we get closer to the mantle. Let's take the word HEART - - if we remove the H and T (H**EAR**T) we come up with the word **EAR.** In order to effectively intercede you must be able to hear.
Once this has been accomplished, remove the H and E (HE**ART**) and we come up with the word **ART.** Intercession is seeking the heart of the Father while using the art to make one free.

The prophetic influence is when we have the mind of the Spirit and are able to communicate the very purpose of our God. If we are going to wait on God continually by keeping mercy, remaining in the place of Prophetic influence, then God is going to have to become our top priority and in many cases our only priority! As a Prophet we are called to keep order, keep judgment, and keep mercy. Keep in mind that when Jonah showed up in the city of Nineveh, he kept judgment as well as divine order. Jonah stated that in forty days God would pour out His wrath and judgment on the city. However, when the people of Nineveh repented Jonah did not remember mercy. The goal of the Prophet is to speak and pray that God will have mercy! Instead of praying for mercy, most of us would rather see wrath because we have failed to maintain that place of mercy. Keep in mind that the sign of a great Prophet is to speak and have it come to pass. Also, the sign of an even greater Prophet is one who lives in the place of intercession that speaks and doesn't have it come to pass, because God has averted it. Why? Because of His mercy! God must keep judgment and order, but He'd rather keep mercy. If people will hear His divine order, recognize the error of their way, and repent, then God will be swift to remember mercy. Notice which comes first – keep mercy and keep judgment.

*That this is a rebellious people, lying children, children that will not hear the law of the Lord. Which say to the Seers, see not; not unto us right things, speak unto us smooth things, prophesy deceits: Get you out of the way, turn aside out of the path, cause the Holy One of Israel to cease from before us.*      *Isaiah 30:9-11*

This is clearly a people that have had their heart seared as with a hot iron. Their hearts are calloused. Remember all the things that happen when one's heart is affected or infected.

## Keep judgment

Adhere to the command and instructions of God coming out of the mouth of His Prophets. The rebellious people rejected and refused the Prophetic influence of their God and the discipline it would bring. The Prophetic speaks of the divine inspiration, divine illumination, divine revelation, divine activation, divine participation, divine intervention, and divine involvement. To reject the Prophetic voice or influence of God is to reject God's active involvement. God wants to be actively involved with His people.

God will raise up individuals in the midst of the assembly, having the Prophetic mantle upon them, having the Prophetic voice, and lifting up the horn. "Lifting up the horn" is a term used to describe those who function and operate in the Prophetic in some way, shape, or form.

Prophetic and Intercessory hearing stems out of the heart. It is so very important that your heart be clean and pure. No Prophet, Seer, or Intercessor can operate with a clouded or closed heart.

*Moreover, David and the captains of the host separated to the service of the sons of Asaph, and of Heman, and of Jeduthun, who should prophesy with harps, with psalteries, and with cymbals: and the number of the workmen according to their service.*     *1 Chronicles 25:1*

*All of these were the sons of Heman, the king's Seer in the words of God, to lift up the horn. And God gave to Heman fourteen sons and three daughters.*     *1 Chronicles 25:5*

If the Prophet, Seer and Intercessor would hear and obey, they would become a Prophetic voice clothed with the same Prophetic anointing while speaking the same Prophetic message. Why doesn't the church have the Prophetic mantle on it? The mantle is a type of vestment that is reserved for the office of the Prophet. Therefore, one receives the mantle and the other receives an anointing that flows off of the mantle.

The church is called to be God's Prophetic voice in this dark world. Remember that the Seer is called to work in connection with the leader. The Prophet is to be God's Prophetic voice and Prophetic influence in the earth, yet the church is to be an anointed Prophetic vehicle that will greatly influence the earth. God has not only set aside a specialized group called a Prophetic people, but through the Spirit of Prophesy, God desires to use the entire church to be a Prophetic influence in the earth. The purpose of the church is to lift up the horn.

*And I fell at his feet to worship Him. And he said unto me, see thou do it not: I am thy fellow servant, and of thy brethren that have the testimony of Jesus: worship God: for the testimony of Jesus is the spirit of prophecy.* **Revelation 19:10**

Through and by this spirit of prophecy, God desires to use the church to bring change in the life of the world. This is where the anointing to prophesy will come on a spirit filled vessel. The important issue is that we remember that this is still not the Seer/Intercessor.

*And the Lord came down in a cloud, and spake unto him, and took up the spirit that was upon him, and gave it unto the seventy elders; and it came to pass that when the spirit rested upon them, they prophesied, and did not cease. ... And Moses said unto him, Enviest thou for my sake? Would God that all the Lord's people were Prophets, and that the Lord would put his spirit upon them.* **Numbers 11:24-29**

There is a great anointing available to all those that are like-minded, or of the same blood type. The same blood type is important if there is to be a continual flow of the Prophetic or the anointing of the Intercessor. The church is God's vehicle of His divine presence.

We are the vessels or channels of and for His divine flow in the earth. The church is called to act as one man, function as one man, and flow as one man. Prophetic people are those who have a Prophetic anointing on them for service. They don't have it on them at all times, yet when the anointing does come on them, it is for service. In order for you and me to wait on God, continually staying under the anointing, we must remain at the place of mediation/intercession and the place of Prophetic influence. Just as you have a right and left hand, you have the gift of intercession and a Prophetic anointing on you, if you are a Seer. To operate in one without the other as a Seer, is to operate using only one hand. To operate in the Prophetic without being an Intercessor is to operate using only one hand.

It is important to understand that intercession is closely tied to the position of the Seer and the source of the prophetic power is found at that place of intimacy with their father. It behooves us to keep in mind that before we can have or release power for God in the prophetic in a public forum, we must first receive power with God in that place of worship and intimacy in the private setting. The greater the Prophet is at the place of worship and fellowship with the Father, Son and Holy Spirit, the greater the impact the Prophet will make when operating in the prophetic.

The greater the Seer is in the place of intercession, the greater they will be in the prophetic flow. Remember the prophetic flow of the Seer is in their seeing and not in speaking. To whom much is given in prophetic seeing, much is required in the place of intercession. There must be a deposit that will come out of us according to the investment made in us.

*And when thou prayest, thou shalt not be as the hypocrites are: for they love to pray standing in the synagogues and in the corners of the streets, that they may be seen of men. Verily I say unto you, they have their reward. But thou, when thou prayest, enter into thy closet, and when thou hast shut thy door, pray to the Father which is in secret; and thy Father which seeth in secret shall reward thee openly.* Matthew 6:5-6

Now in the case where God will choose to use a tag team knowingly or unknowingly, one will do most of the intercession and the other will do most of the prophesying. We have to keep in mind that much of our prophesying is simply the reaping of the anointing from our covering.

There is a great flowing of the anointing off of the Prophet, down on the Seer. The place of intercession is the sowing, and the operating in the Prophetic in a public setting is the reaping. We must remain humble as a Prophetic people and as a seeing/intercessory people, because unless we are given to the place of intercession as well, someone else is doing most of the dirty work for us. We, who are used by God in the prophetic, are used to gain the increase of our God. God has given us seed to sow yet, except we go to the field or the place of reaping, there will not be a harvest. Always keep in mind the price that the Intercessor had to pay before God would ever allow that word to be given or deliverance to be realized.

Everybody wants to be the one that God will use to give the word that brings deliverance but very few are willing to be used by God to be the one who would pay the price for it. Remember the word declares that "many are called but few are chosen". There is a reason that God would say that to the body of Christ, and especially to a body of Seers/Intercessors. There is an investment that must come out of your inner man. It is more than a price – it is an investment. Before there is a smell of fragrance there must come a breaking or a crushing first. The Intercessor, Seer, and the Prophetic person pay their price in a type of "Garden of Gethsemane" (place of crushing). The fragrance or rejoicing can take place now that you have sown or invested yourself in the kingdom.

*And he that reapeth receiveth wages, and gathereth fruit unto life eternal: that both he that soweth and he reapeth may rejoice together. And herein is that saying true, one soweth, and another reapeth. I sent you to reap that whereon ye bestowed no labour: other men laboured, and ye are entered into their labours.* **John 4:36-38**

The key to the power of God that is released in the prophetic is found in the place of intimacy with God through worship. Out of what you see through the flow of personal worship, prophetic intercession is provoked. In the place of personal worship you see the heart of God in a different way. After knowing the endlessness of His grace, you will also come to know the passion that God has for souls and their next place in God. Not only will you come to know that part of God, you will also come to know His endless grace which surpasses the understanding of man. It is not the will of God that any should perish but that all should come to repentance. This is where the art and the power of prophetic worship and intercession come into play.

The power is not in the mechanics of what you do when you prophesy, but it is in the life force behind your prophesying. We want you to not only know how to prophesy, but we also want you to understand the gifts that operate within the prophetic. Yes, it is important to understand the gifts and how to operate in the prophetic, but the problem with most of us is we are only concerned with the mechanics, and not the spirit of life that is supposed to back up what we are doing. There is a form or formula to the approach of the mechanics of our prophesying, but this in operation alone denies the power. Please remember that there is no one, two, or three steps to prophesying, but there is a one-step approach and principle to abide by. The one step approach is the step up into intimacy. Intimacy causes a birthing of the breath of God. You can't have intimacy without worship. It is worship that provokes the prophetic flow. If we say we want the power of God manifested in our lives, yet we never get into a place of worship, we are actually denying the power.

*For men shall be lovers of their own selves, ....*
*Lovers of pleasures more than lovers of God.*
*Having a form of godliness, but denying the power*
*thereof; from such turn away. ... Ever learning,*
*and never able to come to the knowledge of the*
*truth.*                                   *II Timothy 3:1-7*

Jesus said that what we do in private God will reward openly. Now the danger is when we fail to understand that the prophetic gift is a grace gift. The grace gifts can be used by God anytime and anyplace and all that has to happen is for the anointing to flow and that gift will turn on and we will begin to reap where we have applied ourselves. This is called grace gifts because of the empowerment of those gifts. This is Prophetic gifting and **not** the Office of the Prophet. Always keep in mind that the gifts of the Spirit are grace gifts and not fruit, which have to be developed over time, pain, patience, and pressure. Even though there is no need for the gifts themselves to be developed, there is a need for you as the user to be developed before using them. God may use you powerfully in the prophetic gifts, but you are only reaping where you have applied yourself. If you have not applied yourself to be used in the area of these gifts, God will not choose you when it is time for the gift to work. Many of us walk around in spiritual pride because of the prophetic gift that has been turned on, but really we have done nothing to earn it. Intercession will sometime precede the prophetic. Someone occasionally had to pay the price in private if someone else will be used in public. Everyone wants the public life, being seen of men, but very few choose the private life before the Father. The secret to God's power is the private life of preparation, what we do before God and Him alone. It is what we do behind closed doors that count. God will send His power, and honor the vessel that Honors him.

We can't honor Him publicly unless we first honor Him privately. We as Prophets, Prophetic people, and Seers/Intercessors are measured by what we do privately first, not by what we do publicly. God will measure us first in the secret place, not in the place of the open forum. Can you imagine the power that will be released openly when we speak that prophetic utterance, if the power is first released out of our mouth privately in the place of worship and the Intercessor shaking the atmosphere in their private place? If we can keep our hearts right before God, constantly in fellowship with Him, staying in that place of prayer and intercession, there will never be a problem with God using us.

*And Jesus answered them saying, the hour is come, that the son of man should be glorified. Verily, verily I say unto you, except a corn of wheat fall into the ground and die, it abideth alone: but if it die, it bringeth forth much fruit. He that loveth his life shall lose it; and he that hateth his life in this world shall keep it unto life eternal. If any man serve me, let him follow me; and where I am, there shall also my servant be: if any man serve me, him will my Father honor.*
*John 12:23-26*

## Chapter 2
# Prophetic Evangelism

*The word "Prophetic"*
*–adjective*
*1. of or pertaining to a Prophet: Prophetic inspiration.*
*2. of the nature of or containing prophecy: Prophetic*
*writings.*
*3. having the function or powers of a Prophet, as a person.*
*4. predictive; or Prophetic signs; Prophetic warnings.*

T he word Prophetic is a word that bares the nature of prophecy which is to foretell or forth tell; To make a Prophetic declaration or to decree a thing. When we combine this with the word "Evangelism", then we are talking about soul winning with Prophetic manifestations and Prophetic revelation.

The word "Evangelist" is found only three times in the Bible, each in the New Testament and is defined as the one who brings the evangel.

The Evangelist sees the world going to Hell and sees the believer in the pew. He seeks to bring the world into a place of conversion whereby they may have the same experience as the one has had in the pew. The Evangelist's goal is to equip the believer to minister to the sinner.

The Evangelist has a twofold purpose:

1) To bring the revelation of Christ to the sinner, and
2) To bring the revelation and responsibility of equipping, training and evangelizing prophetically to the Prophetic believer,

Evangelism is, at its heart, initiated by the Spirit of God. With that in mind, we can be effective witnesses if we seek to "Move by the Spirit of God" using Prophetic manifestations that look into the heart of the sinner and the Spirit of God which, in turn, will bring conviction (1 Corinthians 14:24-25). The Holy Spirit wants to be involved in our evangelistic efforts. The Evangelist who shares in the oil of the Prophet and the Prophet who shares in the oil of the Evangelist is much more effective and neither is above the other.

The first and foremost purpose of the Spirit of God is to point us to Jesus. The Testimony of Jesus is the Spirit of Prophecy (Revelations 19:10c).

**Who is the Spirit of Prophecy?**

The "Spirit of Prophecy" refers to a manifestation of the HOLY SPIRIT, who conveys Prophetic revelations. **"Holy men of God spake as they were moved by the Holy Ghost" (2 Peter 1:20-21)** It is important to understand that the Holy Spirit is not the Spirit of Prophecy in as much as wisdom is not the Holy Spirit, but a manifestation that He brings. In the same way revelation is not the Holy Spirit, but a manifestation of what the Holy Spirit brings.

Other Expressions:

"The Spirit of Grace"
"The Spirit of Glory"
"The Spirit of Truth"
"The Spirit of Prophecy"
"The Spirit of Revelation
"The Spirit of Wisdom, etc………..

These expressions relate to the Holy Spirit's manifestation
being conveyed through his "Ruach," which is an Aramaic
term that means wind **(Daniel 7:12)** and Spirit of God
**(Daniel 4:8; 5:12).** During the Inter-testament period, the
term Holy Spirit began to replace the term "Spirit" as the
Grace, the Glory, the Truth, the Knowledge, the
Revelation, the Prophecy, etc…

Therefore if we are to understand the Spirit of Prophecy,
we must first not assume that we understand the term
"Spirit." Spirit comes from the same Hebrew word
"ruach," meaning wind, breath or to breathe. The word
used with ruach, however, determines its quality. With that
being said, we could say "the wind of Revelation" or the
"wind of Prophecy," which indicates the utterance came
from God because only God can speak about the future of a
person or thing.

The "Testimony of Jesus" is equated to the Holy Ruach's
(Spirit's) function to inspire the believer with revelation
from God as that believer flows in the oil that rests on the
Prophet to which they are connected. Remember: we flow
in the grace/oil that rests on our Spiritual Father or the
mentor that we are under. **Psalm 133:1-3** talks about the
oil that runs down from Aaron's beard even to his garment.

The oil/grace runs down on us from our Spiritual Father or mentor in the same way.

We should yield to the Holy Spirit's mind as He tells us what to say when evangelizing, because He knows what will convict the people **(1 Corinthians -14:24-25)**. Only a quick (living) Word, Rhema Word, or Prophetic utterance can resurrect the dead. In addition, there is another level of receiving as one that will participate in prophetic evangelism. Prophets function in a "knowing" or, in what I call, Prophetic revelation. An Evangelist or a believer that has the grace of the Prophet on them will have a knowing or Prophetic revelation as well.

This knowing comes by having their senses exercised to discern good from evil or to discern whatever is in the area **(Hebrews 5:14)**. We will find in this season that many will flow in the spirit of Prophetic evangelism that rests on them. Some will not even know what they are flowing in. This will be caused by oil or grace that rests on the ministry or church where they are submitted.

According to **1 Corinthians 14:24,** an unbeliever in the church will be the cause of the release of prophetic utterances. They will become convinced that they are a sinner as the secrets of their hearts are laid bare; so impressed will they be by the supernatural display of knowledge or Prophetic revelation about their private life that he will fall down and worship God, exclaiming that "God is really among you!"

This is the essence of Prophetic Evangelism, in that God will use the gifts of the Spirit (e.g. the Gift of the Word of Wisdom, Word of Knowledge and Discerning of Spirits) in particular ways to capture the attention of unbelievers. This kind of happening will mean that those who function in this area will have to yield to the prophetic prompting of the ministry of the Holy Spirit.

Let's look at some examples of Prophetic Evangelism:

## EXAMPLE # 1:

In **John 4:5-19, 39**, we find dialogue between the woman of Samaria and Jesus. During the communication, Jesus operated in the gift of the Word of Knowledge and through this prophetic revelation, this woman was CONVINCED that Jesus was a Prophet and later that He was the Messiah, the Christ and the Anointed One.

Because Jesus functioned in Prophetic Evangelism, as a result an entire village came to hear Him. One of the reasons is that people want to know what is going on in their life beyond what they are able to see. If we obey the prophetic prompting, we will move back in our places of prophetic dominion that fortune tellers have attempted to take. We are in a season where we are taking dominion of the Prophetic realm or the realm of information. We will talk about that later when we talk about taking dominion over the 7 kingdoms.

Most of Jesus' Ministry of Miracles, Signs and Wonders and the Prophetic took place outside of a religious/church setting. It took place in the streets.

## EXAMPLE # 2:

In **Acts 10:1-44**, we have a story of Cornelius a Roman Centurion, a giving man, a praying man, and an unsaved man. His faithfulness in giving resulted in a "Prophetic

Exchange," a getting of God's attention. God sent an angel to Cornelius, telling him to call for the Apostle Peter, who would minister salvation to him.

(The Angel couldn't do the work of a believer)

Cornelius then sent for Apostle Peter. The next day when they arrived, Peter was in prayer. After the time of prayer, Peter fell into a trance (a manifestation of the Prophetic). During the vision, he saw heaven opening and heard a voice informing him that what God has called clean, he is not to call common. As Peter pondered the vision, the men from Cornelius' house arrived. This is one of the places where Prophetic Evangelism and Prophetic Intercession cross paths. Prophetic Intercession is when you see beyond what things look like now, see the situation as God sees it at the end and you, in earth realm begin to prophetically declare it (there's ruach again). God, therefore, tells Peter what I have cleansed do not call unclean. In other words, God is saying to see it as He sees it and say accordingly.

The Holy Spirit told Peter that there were men arriving and that he was to go with them. Peter went with the men to Caesarea. When He got to Cornelius' house, he preached Christ unto them and Cornelius and his whole house were saved.

I believe we can see that the Spirit of God directed Peter to use the Spirit of Prophecy as he ministered to this Gentile. Peter saw in the realm of the spirit what God saw, said what God was saying and that was a Prophetic utterance. If we are going to flow in Prophetic Evangelism, two things are required:

1) See what God sees and
2) Say what God is saying

When Peter showed up and preached out of his spirit prophetically, God showed out. The Holy Ghost wants to be involved in our Prophetic Evangelistic efforts.

**EXAMPLE # 3:**

In **Acts 16:6**, Paul and his group were forbidden to go into Asia Minor to preach the Gospel. Notice how the Holy Spirit showed Paul a vision of a man in Macedonia calling him there to preach the gospel (see versus 9-10).

**Acts 2:18c - And they shall prophesy……….**

So that we won't read this religiously, let's change the word "prophesy" to its' definition and read it that way. And they shall "speak forth the mind and counsel of God"

**Acts 2:19a— And I will show……………..**

The Holy Spirit desires to guide us in where to go and what to say when we get there, and He'll then confirm the word we <u>speak</u> with signs following.

Consider, **Exodus 4:12– Therefore GO and I will be with thy mouth and teach thee what thou shalt say.**

Before we can share what God shows us, we would have to at least show up and understand that we have power and dominion over nations and kingdoms. Remember much of what you will say has to do with Prophetic Intercession and much of what you do that ends in the salvation of people, is Prophetic Evangelism.

**Romans 10:14a — How then shall they call on him in whom they have not believed?**

**Verse 14b— And how shall they believe in him of whom they have not heard?**

**Verse 14c— And how shall they hear without a preacher?**

**Verse 15— And how shall they preach except they be sent (SEE- MARK 16:15— GO into all the world and Preach the Gospel….)**

**Verse 16— But they have not all obeyed the Gospel, for Isaiah said, Lord, who hath believed our report? How can they hear, if you (the believer) won't GO?**

**Romans 10:17— So then faith comes by hearing and hearing by the word of God.**

They need the "Word from God" that you have in you, spoken to them motivating them to potentially call.

God has given the believer, the ministry of reconciliation, to bear witness that God was in Christ, reconciling the world unto Himself, not imputing their trespasses unto them; and hath committed unto us the word of reconciliation **(2 Corinthians 5:18-20)**.

Now as Prophets, we take this to a whole new dimension through **Malachi 4:6:** which states: **"And he shall turn the heart of the fathers to the children, and the heart of the children to their fathers, lest I come and smite the earth with a curse."**

What are you doing about it?

**Mark 16:15 –...Go YE into all the world and preach the gospel to every creature.**

**Verse 17 - And these signs shall follow them that believe....**

If you really believed, you would GO.

Not every believer is called to stand in the office of the Evangelist or the office of the Prophet, but every believer has a responsibility to evangelize. The believer also has a right to tap into the Prophetic and Evangelistic anointing if they are going to operate in Prophetic Evangelism, but there is a cost to function at that level.

The Evangelistic anointing includes:

1. The Gifts of Healing, the Gift of Faith and the Working of Miracles
2. The ability to win souls
3. The ability to encourage others to evangelize

According to the Apostle Paul, we haven't fully preached Christ, if there isn't a manifestation of signs, wonders, and miracles when needed **(Romans 15:19)**. (Also see Phillip the Deacon, before he became an Evangelist in **Acts 8:5-12)**

As you evangelize, the Holy Spirit will take your God inspired words and reprove the sinner **(John 16:7-9)**.

The word reprove means "convince" or "convict".

**Verse 20 - And they went forth, and preached everywhere, the Lord working with *"them"*, and confirming the word (HIS WORD) with signs following.**

The word *"them"* is italicized, and was not in the original texts. God is not confirming them, But, He is confirming His Word. The Holy Spirit will bring conviction upon the sinner through the (God inspired) words that you speak.

The Prophetic anointing includes:

1. The Gift of Word of Wisdom
2. Word of Knowledge and
3. Discerning of Spirits

They have the responsibility to give prophetic utterances and give prophetic strategies that expose the works of the devil. They uncover what the devil is doing and what he intends to do.

The Holy Spirit is a WITNESS!

**John 15:26 - But when the Comforter is come, whom I will send unto you from the father, even the Spirit of Truth, which proceeds from the Father, He shall TESTIFY of me.** (The Holy Ghost is a WITNESS!)

The Holy Spirit will always point us to Jesus **(Revelation 19:10c)**.

The Holy Spirit can do a work in the heart of the unbeliever that you can't do alone. This is the reason we need Him as our Helper.

**Acts 1:8 - But YE shall receive Power, after that the Holy Ghost is come upon you: And Ye shall be**

**WITNESSES unto me …..** WITNESSES WITH
EVIDENCE OF POWER.

It's obvious, that you will NOT be a WITNESS for Christ,
without the HOLY GHOST. Once He comes to reside on
the inside of you, you will also need Him UP ON you in
order to be effective.

The Holy Ghost and anointing is a WITNESS of what Jesus
provided as an opportunity in Salvation if you are willing
and open to receive it.

**Acts 5:32 - And WE are His WITNESSES of these
things; and so is also the Holy Ghost, whom God hath
given to them that obey him.**

TWO WITNESSES! The Believer and the Holy Ghost!

Jesus' works bore WITNESS of the Father.

When you are doing the works of Jesus and carry it out
with the Holy Ghost and his power, people will know that
God is with you **(John 3:2; Acts 10:38).**

**John 5:36– "But I have a greater WITNESS than that
of John: For the works which the Father hath given Me
to finish, the same works that I do, bear WITNESS of
Me, that the Father hath sent Me".** Remember: the
works we do are always carried out with the Holy Ghost
and power. There must be a manifestation of the Holy
Spirit as we work and even more so in this time as
Prophetic Evangelism is carried out.

Speaking the words of the Father will enable you to be a
powerful WITNESS. The words of the Father are words

filled with prophetic possibility. It is so difficult not to intertwine Prophetic Evangelism with Prophetic Intercession. Why? Because Prophetic Evangelism is reaching out to the lost; while Prophetic Intercession is praying and declaring God's will for the lost as well as those in the body of Christ. The ministry of Jesus is full of examples of both. When you see how Jesus spoke His Father's words, I want you to think of how the prophetic word comes from the Father. In essence, the Word of Wisdom is when God reveals a fragment of His mind to a spirit-filled believer regarding some future event that they could not have known neither on their own nor by natural means.

Jesus only spoke His father's words (Prophetic Words) — **John 12:47-50**

**John 14:10 – "Believe thou not that I am in the Father, and the Father in me? The words that I speak unto you, I speak not of myself: But the Father (Initiator of all Prophetic WORDS) that dwells in me, he does the works".** Remember **"In the beginning was the word and the word was with God, the word was God and all things were made by him." John 1:1.** The Prophetic words you release are filled with creative ability.

Notice something that happened on the day of Pentecost, as Peter preached those God inspired words or Prophetic messages in a preached format. **Acts 2:37 – "Now when they heard this, they were pricked to the heart, and said unto Peter and to the rest of the Apostles, men and brethren, what shall we do?"** Now remember according to **1 Chronicles "the sons of Issachar had understanding of times and knew what Israel ought to do".** Therefore they asked, "what shall we do?" In Prophetic Evangelism, you know what people in your region ought to do.

**Verse 38– Then Peter said unto them, repent, and be baptized every one of you in the name of Jesus Christ for the remission of Sins, and Ye shall receive the gift of the Holy Ghost.** This kind of instruction that ends in a declaration is very prophetic in nature. Remember Peter was not an Evangelist nor was he functioning like one at this point. This was a Prophetic and Apostolic mission at the time which equated to Prophetic Evangelism.

**Verse 41– Then they that gladly received his word were baptized: and the same day there were added unto them about three thousand souls.**

When these men were cut to the heart, they stopped the preaching and asked, "How can we be saved?" While Peter spoke God inspired words or words that were prophetic in nature, the people were convinced by the Holy Ghost. I believe the people that Peter preached to were cut to the heart because Peter's words were sharp and sharp words come emanating from the nature of the Prophet.

**Hebrews 4:12AMP– For the Word that God speaks is ALIVE and full of POWER (Making it active, operative, energizing, and effective.); it is SHARPER than......**

**John 6:63– It is the Spirit the quickens (makes ALIVE) the flesh profits nothing, The words that I speak unto you, they, are spirit and they are LIFE.**

When men and women of God speak words that are inspired of God and they have carried them in their belly as Prophets do, to the degree those words become RHEMA, explosive, and full of creativity to them (real to them) will it yield great results. When the things you speak are not real to you, it has not yet become rhema; therefore, it not yet ready to be spoken. We realize that the whole Bible is inspired of God **(2 Timothy 3:16)** but is the Word alive to you, personally?

**Romans 10:1 - Brethren my heart's desire and prayer to God for Israel is, that they might be saved.**

**Verse 13 - For whosoever shall call upon the name of the Lord shall be saved.**
**Verse 14 - HOW then shall they call on Him in whom they have not believed? And HOW shall they Believe in Him of Whom they have not HEARD? And HOW shall they HEAR without a Preacher?**

**Verse 15 - And HOW shall they Preach, except they be sent? As it is written, how beautiful are the feet of them that preach the Gospel of peace, and bring glad tidings of good things!**

**Verse 16– But they have not all obeyed the gospel. For Esaias saith, Lord who hath believed our report?**

How can the sinner believe if you won't SHOW Up and SHARE what God SHOWS you, enabling Him to SHOW OUT. Our only responsibility in this matter is to say what God tells you to say and do what God tells you to do. He will convince the sinner. He will confirm the word with signs following. Your job is easy; you are simply the messenger.

The Preacher must Go! The Preacher must preach the RHEMA! The Sinner must hear! The sinner must believe! The sinner must call upon the name of the Lord! It's not your words that will do the convincing, it's HIS word, the Word He spoke to you to speak to them. He knows that it

will work! You sow the seed, someone else will water, and God will bring the increase.
You may ask the question: when will I have the chance to go, I work so much and then there is my personal life?

You Preach AS YOU GO **(Matthew 10:7)!**

**Mark 16:15 - Go into all the world and PREACH.** What are you WAITING for? Go! Go! Go!

You can do it! It's easy! God has equipped us with what we need to do the job.

**John 20:21b–..As my father has SENT me, Even so SEND I you.**

**John 8:29 - And He that SENT me is with me: The father has not left me alone; for I do always those things that please Him.** (Faith pleases God Hebrews 11:6)

Remember what Nicodemus said about Jesus, **"NO MAN CAN DO THESE MIRACLES EXCEPT GOD BE WITH HIM" John 3:2**

Jesus was not alone. The Father (the Sender) was with Him. He that SENT us is with us also.
**John 5:19b** Paraphrased - **"I only do those things I SEE my Father Do."** How could Jesus, SEE His Father doing anything? Did He have some special crystal ball? NO! He saw His Father's Works in the form of the Word. The Father and The Word are One!

**John 12:49-50 - For I have not spoken of myself; but the Father which SENT me, He gave me a commandment,**

**(WORD) what I should SAY, and what I should SPEAK.**

**Verse 50 - And I know that His commandment is life everlasting: Whatsoever I speak therefore, Even as the father said unto me, so I speak.**

**John 14:10 – Believest thou not that I am in THE FATHER and THE FATHER in me? The WORDS that I SPEAK unto you I SPEAK not of myself: But THE FATHER that dwelleth in me, He doeth THE WORKS.** Let the Word do the Work! The Word Works!

If you are sent by God to preach the gospel to those of whom you come into contact with daily, and you are if you are a believer, then speak the Word of God.

PREACH simply means to proclaim out loud the gospel.

You may not have a collar; you may not have a license; you may not have a certificate on the wall; you may not be standing in the office of a ministry gift; but you do have a responsibility to share the gospel with those you come into contact with daily.

Your license to do that is **MARK 16:15**.

**John 3:34 - He that God hath SENT SPEAKS the WORDS of GOD.**

## Chapter 3

# Prophetic Intercession

**2 Peter 1:21 - For the prophecy of old time came not by the will of man, but Holy men of God spake as they were moved by the Holy Ghost.**

These Prophets, (or Holy Men of God, as they were known) spake as they were inspired by the Holy Spirit, or we can say as the Holy Spirit gave them utterance. (2 Timothy 3:16; Acts 2:4)

If men can speak by the prompting of the Holy Ghost, then they can pray by the prompting of the Holy Ghost. Men can be inspired to pray. Men can pray as the Holy Ghost gives them utterance.

*And they were all filled with the Holy Ghost and began to speak with other tongues, as the spirit gave them utterance.*        *Acts 2:4*

In this chapter our focus will be Prophetic Intercession, speaking forth the will of God in prayer. In fact, the most effective kind of prayer is the prayer that the Holy Spirit inspires at the moment.

We will first define some key words that will enable us to see what the Holy Ghost is saying on this subject more clearly.

Prophetic is defined as: that which has the nature and characteristics of prophecy. However that doesn't tell us much if we don't know the definition of the word prophecy. Prophecy, Prophesy, and Prophesying come from the Greek word- "Propheteia". The Greek prefix "PRO" is defined as "FORTH" and the word "Phemi" is defined as "to speak" So then Propheteia is defined as - To Speak Forth!

The Vines Expository Dictionary defines Prophecy as to speak forth the mind and counsel of God. It appears that this definition has packaged the Revelation Gifts and the Gift of Prophecy in one package. We need to appreciate that terms can be used both generally and specifically. Specifically speaking, the Gift of Prophecy is edification, exhortation, and comfort (**1 Corinthians 14:3**). Generally speaking, prophecy includes all three of the Inspiration Gifts. The Inspiration Gifts: Gift of Prophecy, Gift of Tongues and the Gift of Interpretation of Tongues are listed among the gifts of the Spirit outlined in **1 Corinthians 12**.

Let's start with defining the Revelation Gifts.

**The Gift of the Word of Wisdom** – It is a supernatural revelation of the mind and purpose of God given to man for a specific purpose. This is the gift that points to the future. This is the gift that many call prediction.

**The Gift of the Word of Knowledge** – It is a supernatural revelation of any event or fact, given to us for a specific purpose. This gift points to the present or the past.

**The Gift of Discerning of Spirits** – It is a supernatural revelation of the presence and activities of the spirit realm giving us the ability to see into the spirit realm. Enabling the individual to have spiritual visions, and open visions.

*Utterance Or Inspiration Gifts*

**The Gift Of Prophecy** – It is a supernatural utterance inspired by God in your known language, exhorting, comforting, and edifying. (This is not a revelation gift.) The Gift of Prophecy is PROPHECY specifically speaking and the Revelation Gifts are PROPHECY generally speaking.

The Revelation Gifts REVEAL something, while the Utterance Gifts SAY something

So then, we can see that Prophecy is both Forth-telling and Fore-telling. Prophecy is speaking the word of God under the anointing whether it is applicable to the past, present or future. One of the ways of accessing the mind and counsel of God is through prayer; which brings us to our next term - Intercession

As we discuss Prophetic Intercession. The Hebrew Word for INTERCESSION is PAGA and is defined as to meet with an outcome, or a meeting with an outcome. "Paga" represents one of the strongest Old Testament words for asking. It's also used to describe a violent meeting.

Note: Another word for ask is to demand! When we speak and act on the word of God, we are placing a demand on the anointing. We are placing a demand on what rightfully belongs to us.

**Matthew 11:12** says that the violent takes what rightfully belongs to him by force.

*Job 6:25 says "How Forcible are right words" and Psalm 33:4 say's "The Word of the Lord is RIGHT.*

When we put these thoughts together we find that as we speak forth God's word in prayer, we apply a violent force to the situations and circumstances that oppose the will of God for our lives and simultaneously place a demand on the anointing to perform in our lives, or those we are interceding for.

*Intercession - Also comes from the Greek word "Enteuxis", which means:*

    *a.  To meet with in order to Converse*
    *b.  To seek the presence and hearing of God on behalf of others*
    *c.  Standing in the Gap in Prayer-in-Between a person(s). Intercession is under the unction and promptings of the Holy Ghost*
    *d.  Advocate*
    *e.  Mediator (Heb.)*
    *f.  Days man (Heb. term) Job 9:33*

With all of this seeking and meeting going on, we have placed ourselves in a position to hear the mind and counsel of God, and speak forth that wisdom in prayer as the Lord directs us.

**This is Prophetic Intercession!**

*Prophetic Action and Declaration:*

Prophetic Intercession has to do with us as Prophetic people moving in the realm of Intercession from a Prophetic standpoint. Then we have Prophetic Action and

Declaration that releases God in a situation or area. When God wants to do something, he gets a Prophet in whom he has given regional or national authority over a land to speak forth prophetically.

What is Prophetic?

1) Foretelling, speaking about something in the future that God has decreed will come to pass.
2) Forth telling, speaking something forth for God, or becoming his voice in the earth. Usually that is something we call preparatory, when He tells a Prophet to speak

There are three reasons we release something in the earth:

1) Obedience to God brings a response from God. God sometimes requires something from us in order to receive what He said he would do. God requires a Prophetic act and a Prophetic declaration. There are moments of obedience that God requires for us to do something He has released. We don't always know why God wants us to do something, He just wants it done. Naaman was told to go dip in the Jordan seven times without any further explanation, yet he was expected to obey that Prophetic act.

Examples of Prophetic Acts:
a. Moses at the Red Sea was told to lift his rod - that was a Prophetic act.
b. Moses again was told to put his rod up and as long as the rod remained up, Israel won the battle or prevailed, but when it came down they began to lose; Exodus 17. That was a Prophetic

act. Hear the principle of how this Prophetic
Act works: You do something in the earth
realm, God does something in the heavenly
realm and there is a manifestation that happens
in the earth realm. This is that seed sowing
principle or the principle of reciprocity. What
we do is in obedience to God, and then heaven
can respond, causing something in the earth
realm to happen. The principle is this; there is
something happening in the spirit realm that
cannot be broken until earth obeys. The Rod
represented the delegated authority in the earth
and Moses was to lift up the Rod that
represented the authority of God. When that
happened, Israel prevailed. When it was not
lifted up, Israel was beginning to be defeated.

c. Prophetic Declarations: Thou shalt make thy
prayer unto him, and he shall hear thee, and
thou shalt pay thy vows. Thou shalt also decree
a thing, and it shall be established unto thee: and
the light shall shine upon thy ways. Job 22:27-
28, there is something about decreeing things in
the earth that causes heaven to establish it.

2) Faith releases God. Hope and Faith Are Partners

If your hope is bigger than your faith then you can
strain your faith trying to reach your hope that you
are not developed for. Creating a hope or an image
in your thinking that someday you would like to
achieve will assure that you will come into it if you
apply faith principles with it.

You must start with where you are in reference to
your faith. What I mean by that is you have to
identify where or what level your faith is already

working and then start at that point believing and developing.

If we will have "The God kind of faith" we will need to go back to the faith teaching of Jesus and seeing God and how He functioned in his faith operation. Since Jesus is saying to us "have faith in God" or have the God kind of faith then it is obvious that the kind of faith Jesus used was the same kind that God used. If Jesus said the "God kind of faith", then are there other kinds? Yes!

What kinds of faith photos are there:

    a. Great Faith-**Matthew 8:5-10**
    b. Little Faith-**Matthew 14:22; Luke: 12:28**
    c. Weak Faith -**Romans 4:19**
    d. Strong Faith- **Romans 4:20**
    e. No Faith-**Mark 4:40**
    f. Dead Faith-**James 2:20**
    g. Unfeigned Faith- **1Timothy 1:5**

We have been created with the God kind of faith originally, but lost it when Adam sinned. The good news is, Jesus redeemed us and the God kind of faith was restored in us. In the book of **Romans 12: 3** …but God hath dealt to every man the measure of faith.

Let's look at how the God Kind of Faith works:

*And on the morrow, when they were come from Bethany, he was hungry: And seeing a fig tree afar off having leaves, he came, if haply he might find anything thereon: and when he came to it, he found nothing but leaves; for the time of figs was not yet. And Jesus answered and said unto it, No man eat fruit of thee hereafter forever. And his disciples heard it.*

**Mark 11:12-14**

1) Jesus had a Need/Desire-"he was hungry"
2) He saw the answer to his Need-"Seeing a fig tree afar off"
3) Jesus set his expectation to Receive-"He came if haply he might   find anything there on"
4) Jesus spoke to what did not produce- "No man eat fruit of thee here after forever"
5) He set his expectation again on what he said next and made sure he was heard

There are several components that are necessary for you to function at the level of production.

1. Diligence: you must be diligent in your assignment that God gives you and in what God says to you. One of the greatest pitfalls of potential faith walkers is they are tempted to side step or not continue in their faith-filled actions. Remember: Faith is Acting on what you believe. There has to be a continuing of the initial steps of faith.
2. Eliminate Faith Enemies: You have to have a holy lifestyle and not tolerate faith's enemies. Many people walk and talk faith, but live a compromising lifestyle that causes faith not to work. Some of faith's enemies include: works of the flesh, lust of the flesh, pride of life and lust of other things entering in choke the Word and makes the Word of faith unfruitful.

When God dealt with me about the miracle of the "Empty Envelope" I did not think of it as a miracle happening, more than I did have the thought of wanting to give into something that I could not give into. What you make happen for others, God makes happen for you.

Knowing that some would need to copy this process, I thought it prudent to give you some steps:

    a. Name Your Seed's Directions - (You have to want to give into something away from you, in order to change your financial picture.) What if you believe for something else? Your faith still needs a target. What is the object of your faith?

*Isaiah 55: For as the rain cometh down, and the snow from heaven, and returneth not thither, but watereth the earth, and maketh it bring forth and bud, that it may give seed to the sower, and bread to the eater: So shall my word be that goeth forth out of my mouth: it shall not return unto me void, but it shall accomplish that which I please, and it shall prosper in the thing whereto I sent it.*

        a. Name your amount on the envelope before saying anything.
        b. Know how much you can believe for not how much you would like to believe for.

   c. Declare aloud what you believe based on your reason for giving this offering.

   d. Establish your foundation which makes this true (2 Corinthians 9:10 Now he who gives seed to the sower.)

   e. Cast the care of this on God.

   f. Realize that what you believe for may come little by little or in one lump.

   g. Don't tell God where or how to bring it in.

   h. Based on all the above, release your faith on this.

   i. Establish corresponding action.

3) Speaking God's Word releases His creativity that lives in the word spoken.

What is real Prophetic Intercession? Prophet's don't intercede as Intercessors would. Intercessors go to God on behalf of the people, but Prophets go the people on behalf of God. The Prophets order never changes. Therefore, when the Prophet makes the declaration that he or she is told by God to make in the earth the people, the region or that nation shifts, the Prophet is told to speak to get the benefit. The Prophetic declaration or Prophetic Intercession is when Prophets speak into the atmosphere and something happens.

Let's look at Ezekiel's example of Prophetic Intercession:

"The hand of the LORD was upon me, and carried me out in the Spirit of the LORD, and set me down

in the midst of the valley which was full of bones,
And caused me to pass by them round about: and,
behold, there were very many in the open valley;
and, lo, they were very dry. And he said unto me,
Son of man, can these bones live? And I answered,
O Lord GOD, thou knowest. Again he said unto
me, Prophesy upon these bones, and say unto them,
O ye dry bones, hear the word of the LORD"

**Ezekiel 37:1-4** This is a clear example of Prophetic
Intercession. Look closely **"The hand of the
LORD was upon me, and (1) carried me out in
the Spirit of the LORD, and (2) set me down in
the midst of the valley which was full of bones,
And (3) caused me to pass by them round about:**
This is what I call the threefold preparation process
of Prophetic Intercession. (1) God carried Ezekiel
out in the Spirit of the Lord where he could see
from a different vantage point. Many times we try
to see from where we understand in our thinking
which could be only in the first dimension, but God
wants us to see from the realm of the spirit. We
have to see things from their vantage point in order
for us to effective. (2) God set Ezekiel down in the
midst of that situation that he was going to speak.
Unless Ezekiel, you or I come in the midst of that
situation, we cannot speak to it as one that will
intercede prophetically, that is, to prophetically
declare a thing unless we are in it speaking from the
inside. If we are called to youth we have to get in
the realm where they are and feel what they feel in
order to pray from their vantage point. (3) God
caused Ezekiel to pass by it round about. God
wanted Ezekiel to see the situation from every side
and not miss any possible angle of intercession or

speaking to it prophetically. You and I cannot possibly speak to a nation that we have no information on.

God has always given Prophets information about the nation He wanted them to speak to. Verse seven said "So I prophesied as I was commanded: and as I prophesied, there was a noise, and behold a shaking, and the bones came together, bone to his bone".

Therefore, Ezekiel prophetically declared to that nation what God said or health and healing could not come to it (**Ezekiel 37:7**). It must be understood that just anybody cannot prophetically intercede for a city, region or nation. You have to be called to an assignment. Sometimes God calls a church or a group of people to a particular assignment and as a corporate body we would have to do that assignment together; prophetically declare to that nation what God is saying. Remember: the Prophet has the ability to release God's creative ability in that nation or situation where others don't have the ability to release the same thing.

Prophet Isaiah was given an assignment to prophetically declare into a certain nation. Isaiah, while he was in the midst of prophesying, paused the prophecy to declare "I will say to the north, Give up; and to the south, Keep not back: bring my sons from far, and my daughters from the ends of the earth; Even every one that is called by my name: for I have created him for my glory, I have formed him; yea, I have made him". We have to see that God has given us Intercessory power and authority to speak to the nations or at least to our region. This is Prophetic Intercession. Not everyone has the authority to speak on the own behalf.

## Chapter 4

# The Prophet and Deliverance

Within the general makeup of the Prophet is the gift of discerning of spirits. This is, or should be, a gift that flows out of the Prophetic person. The gift of discerning of spirits, along with the other eight gifts of the Spirit, should be manifested in the life of the Prophet, the Prophetic minister, and occasionally those who function in Prophetic gifting. It is the gift of discerning of spirits that will enable the Prophet to see, supernaturally, the plans, purpose, and working of the enemy and its' force. Also, the gift of discerning of spirits will give the Prophet the ability to see in the realm of the spirit in order to clearly understand the maneuvering and the functioning of the spirit that is in operation and that is given physical manifestation at that time.

We need to look beyond what we see in order to recognize the plan, purpose and working of the enemy. We do this with the gift of discerning of spirits. The enemy has a plan to talk you out of obeying God and start doubting God. The enemy wants to stop the flow of what God is doing. The gift of discerning of spirits is not discerning what people are doing but discerning the operation of spirits. God will reveal particular spirits and not just tell people's business. Sometimes people are afraid of coming in the presence of a

Prophet because they have the misunderstanding that God
is going to tell the Prophet all of their business and he or
she is going to tell everybody, especially if they know that
they have some things in their lives that they need to
change. God is not a gossiper and what He reveals He
intends to heal. The Prophets and some Prophetic people
are able to discern particular spirits, seeing in the spirit, and
are able to know the plan, purpose and working of the
enemy. And they can attack these plans, purposes and
workings of the enemy and not people.

*To another the working of miracles; to another prophecy,
to another discerning of spirits, to another divers kinds of
tongues and to another the interpretation of tongues.*
*I Corinthians 12:10*

**Mark 9: 4-29** is the account of the physical manifestation
of a deaf and dumb spirit that had possessed the young boy
who was brought to the Lord Jesus by his father for
deliverance. Let us take a look at some possible
manifestations of a deaf and dumb spirit and how it would
manifest itself at particular levels of oppression and
possession. This example in **Mark 9** is possession. But this
spirit may not always be in the form of possession. It may
come in the form of oppression. Possession is the total
control by a demonic force over an individual's soul (mind,
will, emotion, imagination and intellect). Oppression is a
force that would come against or attack the mind and/or the
flesh. Oppression works from the outside. It is more
emotional than spiritual.

It is the role and responsibility of the Prophet to recognize
and/or identify the various levels of spiritual and demonic
influence within the congregation. It is important not to
call what may be a work of the flesh demonic or what may
be demonic a work of the flesh. We must identify what the

works of the flesh are and must not attempt to cast out what is not demonic.

The person operating in the works of the flesh (**Galatians 5:17-21**) is not necessarily demonic. The individual must take authority and control over their own flesh, bringing it into subjection to their recreated or born-again spirit. This begins the developing of babes in Christ versus someone who continually walks in the flesh. The Prophet would have to discern this area because of his authority to correct and/or chastise the body. Those that are babes will find themselves wrestling with their flesh. Once again, this does not mean that it is a demonic influence.

### *Recognizing Demonic Influence*

We must be able to recognize the various stages of demonic influence. There are six stages:

1. **Regression** – Regression is to withdraw or to back away from. We should be able to discern this stage within the midst of our congregation. People who begin to become isolated from the body are in the stage of regression.

One of the ways to identify people who are headed out of the back door of the church is by their acts of regression toward the back of the church. This demonic activity causes them to be incapable of communicating. You have to go after them. You will notice that they will begin to change their seat from wherever they normally sit to a little farther back each time they come to church. The next time they come, they stop talking to people and will not say anything to anyone. They are literally backing their way out of the back door. This is the time when you go after them because you recognize the signs and they are not able to communicate with you. These are the beginning stages of demonic influence of regression.

## When is this regression and when is this Prophetic preparation?

Regression does not allow you to interact with others. However, regressing Prophetically will not prevent your interaction but will cause conflict in forcing interaction because of your season.

Regression also has a prophetic side. Regression is a prophetic act when you sense in your spirit that God is doing something with you prophetically that you cannot have interference with. At this time you begin to regress, and you really need to do that. You need to get away from people who will interfere with your process of receiving from God at this time. This does not mean that you are angry with anyone; you can talk to people and communicate with people. There are no demonic forces involved because you are not hindered from communicating; you are choosing to separate yourself so that you can receive from God.

2. **Suppression** – Suppression is manifested from lack of joy. A person begins to hide his or her feelings and is unable to express joy.

To suppress is to keep from being revealed, or to inhibit the expression of something. The Prophet must be mindful of what he talks about or confesses. Men do this from time to time (suppressing things), especially married men. This is a dangerous thing to do because this act of suppression leads you to the next stage of depression. This demonic influence is leading you to a place of losing control and that is not what God wants to happen to us. Most of the healthy people just go off every time something happens; they do not suppress anything.

Prophetically, we use suppression to control the flow of information. This is prophetic preparation. Suppression is different. Suppression is denying what one feels.

3. **Depression** – Depression is a broken spirit. People are not able to overcome the things in their lives. God has been speaking to you through all of these previous stages. Now, He is saying, Come out of this. At this stage, you have started to follow the demon out of the presence of God, and God wants you to come out now because this leads you to the next phase of oppression. You cannot carry some things because you are not designed to do that. God wants to carry that care for you. The only thing that you are designed to carry is the word of God and the glory of God.

If depression not arrested, caught or put in check at this point, depression will lead to oppression, which opens the door to possession. Depression is a period of drastic decline. There is that time when the Prophet goes into a desert place, but never a drastic decline.

4. **Oppression** – Oppression describes one who is weighed down with the cares of this world. Oppressed people lack victory. At this stage, people cannot remember any of their victories in their lives. This shuts down the voice of God.

Oppression is to keep down by unjust use of authority, or to weigh heavily on the mind or spirit (**1 Corinthians 7:37; 2 Corinthians 9:7 NIV or NASB**). The prophetic side of oppression is called discipline. Your flesh is being oppressed. Discipline is training expected to produce a specific character or pattern. School is the place of discipline and challenge.

5. **Obsession** – Obsession describes one who lacks reality. Obsessed individuals become focused on one particular sin in their life. At this stage, they are not functioning the way that God created them.

Obsession is defined as a compulsive, often unreasonable idea or emotion, or an irresistible impulse to act on an unreasonable idea, problem or thing. This quality should be on the Prophet in a positive sense. It should happen in a time of preparation.

6. **Possession** – A person experiencing possession is someone who comes under total control of a demonic force.

In our prophetic preparatory period, we should come under the control of the Holy Spirit, which involves being totally submitted to Him (**1 Corinthians 16:14-16**). They have addicted themselves to the ministry of the saints.

## The Spirit of Perversion

Homosexuals are bound with the spirit of perversion. The word perversion means to deviate from the original form. There are men who are bound by that spirit that have never entered into a homosexual relationship. Likewise, people who are bound with that spirit make a choice to leave their natural use.

The first five of these stages are mental and emotional harassment by the enemy. The sixth is spiritual, a total yielding of the person's soul to a demonic force. All of these stages, through the gift of discerning of spirits, can be discerned, and the person can be delivered.

## The Prophet's Role in Discernment

Through the Prophet's spiritual insight, his or her ability to discern spiritual influence is great. Within the Prophet's role and responsibilities in ministry, there will be times during impartation that it is necessary for him to be cognizant of various levels of demonic influence, oppression and/or possession. The Prophet may, from time to time, discern, cast out and/or deliver an individual from whatever level of demonic influence present.

### *Particular Spirits and How They Manifest*

**Mark 1:21-28 A Religious Spirit** – The manifestation of this unclean spirit seemed to have a revelation of who Jesus was and a religious knowledge that would allow him to fit in with most religious people. The remedy: Jesus prophetically discerned the spirit and its function and commanded it to hold its peace and come out of the man.

**Mark 5:1-19 A Spirit of Insanity** – The manifestation of this unclean spirit was able to tap into a portion of this man's mind and cause him to have incredible strength. This is a man who manifested multiple personalities through the influence of a demonic spirit that brought much damage to his body. But, at a spare break from demonic activity, he, in the presence of Jesus, fell down and worshipped Him. This was a clear indication that showed an act on the man's part that he wanted to be delivered.

The scriptures can help us identify the difference between a demonic spirit and a sickness. When Jesus was in the presence of sickness, there was not a spiritual or physical reaction. But when He was in the presence of demonic influence, there was a manifestation or a reaction within the person. Both physical and spiritual are present. The demonic spirit responds with a physical manifestation.

The gift of discerning spirits is one of the many gifts within the body of Christ. *"Now ye are the body of Christ and members in particular."* Are you sure that you can recognize **"the realms of prophecy"? (1 Corinthians 12:27)**

## Chapter 5

# Prophetic Faith Concepts

It is important to understand the types of faith concepts that directly affect the Prophet's office. There may be more, but these are the ones we will deal with:

- Giving as a principle
- Receiving
- Declaring against all odds
- Decreeing a thing
- Functioning where you have no points of reference and lastly
- Calling those things that are not as though they are.

### Three Types of Giving

Many Prophets desire to walk in all of the blessings of God yet they have not understood how to tap into that place which unlocks abundance. Most of us as Prophets don't function in giving ourselves as a principle. We want others to do what we don't do by principle. Giving is one of those areas that we don't practice what we preach. God dealt with me at one point as I sought to understand wealth principles. I was one that tithed and gave offerings as I was able to do so.

Then one day I came to understand three powerful principles that set me free financially. And my assignment is to teach it to those that desire to come out of financial bondages and break through the financial barriers they are in. And yes there is an anointing on this giving message! The anointing being, that which destroys bondages. If it did not break or destroy a yoke or bondage it was not anointed.

### Systematic Giving

This is when you give by a system that is already established or will be. Tithing is God's system for security and blessing. You have to cooperate with the system by tithing and giving offerings.

This giving plan is found over in the book of **Malachi 3:10**:

*"Bring ye all the tithe into the storehouse, that there may be meat in mine house, and prove me now herewith, saith the Lord of hosts"...*                    *Malachi 3:10*

When anyone systematically participates God will automatically do several things:

a. Open the windows of heaven
b. Pour out a blessing too large to receive at one time
c. Will rebuke the devourer for you and
d. Bring your harvest in its time.

God said He would do all of these things because of what we do systematically with the tithe and offerings. We must understand that this must be done on a regular consistent basis. Systematic giving is like an insurance plan, as long as you pay your premium, you and all your stuff are covered. When your payments go lacking, the policy is in default and there are consequences.

**Spontaneous Giving**

This form of giving occurs when there is an unexpected request made. There are times that we come to a point in our life where God is asking for something from us we had not planned for. You have to understand this is what makes it spontaneous giving. Now this kind of giving accesses something in the earth realm that is over and above the regular yet not "Supernatural". **Luke 6:38** says: *"Give and it shall be given unto you; good measure, pressed down, and shaken together, and running over, shall men give into your bosom."* This is not accessing the supernatural realm in your giving though this is nice. Men at this point of giving are charged to start looking for you to give to you. Spontaneous giving always will attract mankind to give to you. This is a law that we have tapped into and many don't understand how this law works. So when the opportunity presents itself many don't move on it. What is the difference then between systematic giving and spontaneous giving? The difference is systematic giving is your managing what belongs to God and therefore God rewards your faithfulness. Whereas spontaneous giving is giving out of what you don't have to give. However you are participating in an investment opportunity that causes men to be driven to give to you.

**Sacrificial Giving**

Now this is the type of giving that accesses the supernatural realm in its return. We see this giving plan operating many times in the Bible. In **1Kings 17** the widow woman was selected by God to provide for Elijah yet her position was not conducive for that kind of situation. Think about who she had to take care of: Elijah, the baby, herself and her household. What made it supernatural? The return coming instantly and over time made it supernatural. What made it a sacrifice? Because it was all she had and it was to go to her man of God as a first fruit offering which made it a sacrifice. By principle God does not glory in someone's last, but does glory in someone's first. Now this is why most people don't come into a supernatural harvest: either they give their last, or maybe their man of God does not permit them. This is the breaker on both sides. The man of God suffers by seeing you give your last and doesn't want to receive it, or you want to hold on to your last. This is a principle that I worked to increase in my life when I was working for almost nothing.

**Examples of Sacrificial Giving:**

- The lad with the fish and the loaves
- The widow with the cruise of oil

**2 Corinthians 9:6-8** set the stage for our understanding the giving process and under what plan we desire to enter. The choice has always been ours. We have said, "When God wants to bless us, He will" however nothing could be further from the truth. God has always put our financial future in our hands. We have just either out of ignorance or out of an unwilling heart decided we were not going to cooperate with the giving plan. **2 Corinthians 9:6-8** in the Amplified Bible says:

*"Remember this: he who sows sparingly and grudgingly will also reap sparingly and grudgingly, and he who sows generously that blessings may come to someone will also reap generously and with blessings. Let each one give as he has made up his own mind and purposed in his heart, not reluctantly or sorrowfully or under compulsion for God loves (he takes pleasure in, prizes above other things, and is unwilling to abandon or to do without, a cheerful (joyous, prompt to do it) giver whose heart is in his giving. And God is able to make all grace (every favor and*

*earthly blessing) come in abundance, so that you may always and under all circumstances and whatever the need be self-sufficient [possessing enough to require no aid or support and furnished in abundance for every good work and charitable donation]." 2 Corinthians 9:6-8 AMP*

# – PROPHETIC EXCHANGE –

**Philippians 4:10** describes the Prophetic Exchange. Prophetic Exchange is when you let those who are over your life spiritually (pastor, mentor or covering) receive of your natural things so that you can receive of their spiritual things (anointing, gifts, grace and oil).

When I sensed the level of revelation that was on some of those that I was tapped into in the various seasons of my growth, I made sure there was a Prophetic Exchange that took place. What that means is, I give to them of my natural things (treasure, time and/or talent) and I have a right to receive from them (anointing, oil, gifts, grace and favor). I have a right to receive from you if I sow into you. What is it that we receive? What is it that Paul received? Paul received relief, financial relief, from the church of Philippi and often times he received of their time. They then had a right to the grace that was on his life, to walk in his grace and favor.

Jesus said, "My grace is sufficient for thee; My strength is made perfect in weakness." We want to grab hold of that, but He was not talking to us. He was talking to Paul, because Paul had matured to a particular level. And Jesus said, "No, Paul, I am not going to do this for you. You do this for you." And He said, "My grace, Paul, is sufficient for thee." He was really teaching Paul: "Those that are coming up in ranks behind you, Paul, those that you are pouring into, wait until you see that they have matured to a certain level, and then say, 'My grace that's on me, which is the grace that Jesus put on me, is sufficient for you.'" So that is a Prophetic Exchange.

You can't buy it; it is not for sale. It is a reciprocal system: when you give of your natural things, it is an exchange that comes back to you in a Prophetic release, or the things that you need in your spiritual life. So Paul declares particular things, he says you have passageway now. You can enter in; it is your choice. I want to urge you that all God has prepared, you and I can enter into, but we have to want this.

I will never forget when I was at Jericho. Apostle Betty, whom we affectionately knew as Mom Betty, did not know that I had said this. Out of a thousand or so people, I watched her and Bishop Peebles, and I said "I want that, that supernatural ability that they have and the level of revelation, I want that. Whatever it takes, I want it. Whatever they know, I want that". Every book that they talked about, I purchased. Every Bible they mentioned, I purchased. I had to believe the money in because I had to have that. I would not leave out of there without purchasing a tape. I wanted what was on them. I had to know it. I made a sacrifice. I gave up all those pleasures and pastimes, "I gave it all up, God, and I want that. I need this." God said, "Rodney, Prophetic Exchange. What do you give? What are you going to give?" I will make every possible sacrifice, because I do want it. Money is not dear to me; I want that. What will you give for that which you desire to tap into? "I sell out to you, God." I have to have that costly anointing.

Just the normal church life was not good enough for me. You have to get to the place where the normal church life is not good enough for you. Just to walk as a mere human that has gone through church, that's not good enough. I'm selling out to you right now, Father. I sell out to you. This, I have to have: divine ability to do anything. I need divine ability to tap in there.

I watched this anointing on two people. Bishop Peebles would run by people -- healing and deliverances would take place just because he ran by. "God, I want that." "Rodney, are you willing to pay the price?"

Everything else is secondary. You have to make God your choice. You have to decide to put sin down, and make God your choice.

There is a tremendous cost. Are you willing to pay that cost? Just the norm is not good enough. I have to have more. I need manifestation.

God spoke to me: "Rodney, if you want all that you say you want, sell out to Me." "What do you mean, sell out?" "Give it all up. Rodney work for Me. That means you have to give Me your will. That means when you want to, and I don't want you to, you can't." I had to fight "me" on occasion. I decided, God, I want all of you. I want to receive it. And I realize it comes through Prophetic Exchange.

God, if you give me the anointing, I can do this. The anointing answers all. What is it that you feel like you can't do? Receive the anointing. Receive the anointing. Sell out to God. It doesn't matter where you are right now, sell out to God.

## Chapter 6

# Prophetic Dominion (7 Kingdoms)

The levels of prophetic jurisdiction, influence and prophetic authority of the prophetic arm are identified based on the prophet type that frequents your life.

### The Prophet to the Nations: 1Kings 18: 17-24

This Prophet has the ability to see into the nation(s) that has been assigned to him. This Prophet has a word to nations and kingdoms in addition; he/she has several realms of authority:

1. National and International Authority: This is the kind of authority that Jesus attempted to teach his disciples in the book of Mark 4th chapter. I question whether we as Prophetic people 1) really understand this level of "authority" and 2) are we even sensitive to what our assignment is.

2. National and International Insights:

*"And of the children of Issachar, which were men that had understanding of the times, to know what Israel ought to do"* **1 Chronicles 12:32**
Do you know what your region, church or nation ought to do? If you are called to that region you should know.

3. National and International Sensitivity to Seasons and Times: **Hebrews 5:11-14**

4. National and International Dominion over Kingdoms and Nations: **1Kings 18: 21-24**

Lucifer's region became Adam's

Introduction

1) Why has God selected you to operate in the Prophetic, and
2) What is your place in God by way of assignment?

Many of us, as Prophets and Prophetic people, are not producing at the level that God wants us to produce, and the reason that we don't is because we do not know who we really are, nor do we understand why God has selected us and why the enemy hates us. I am convinced that in times past we only thought we knew who we were, but once we get through today, you will know who you are and why the enemy hates you so much.

**Genesis 1:1-2: "In the beginning God created the Heaven and the earth. And the earth was without form, and void; and darkness was upon the face of the deep. And the Spirit of God moved upon the face of the waters." (KJV)** From this passage we can see that in the beginning, God created the heaven and the earth. This is the period before history. This was the time of the cavemen and dinosaurs, etc. In the beginning, God did, then billions of years passed. When we notice that the earth was without form and void and the darkness was upon the face of the deep, we know that this condition is not beautiful, nor is it perfect. Does God create things in that condition? Let's find out from:

**Deuteronomy 32:4 His way is perfect.** How we see it in Genesis is not perfect.

**Ecclesiastes 3:11: "He hath made everything beautiful in his time: also he hath set the world in their heart, so that no man can find out the work that God maketh from the beginning to the end."** THE EARTH WAS BEAUTIFUL

Notice that this passage lets us know that God had made everything beautiful. Everything that God makes is beautiful. You are beautiful because everything that God makes is beautiful. When He created the earth, it was beautiful. The earth was a marvelously beautiful place when God created it. In the beginning God did it; He created the heaven and the earth, then billions of years passed. Adam at that time was not here.

►Process is that key that brings preeminence.
The word "preeminence" means "highly distinguished or outstanding, standing out among all others because of superiority in a field or activity". We will never stand out or be distinguished from anyone else if we don't go through the process that brings it on.

**Mark 1:10-13**
**And straightway coming up out of the water, he saw the heavens opened, and the Spirit like a dove descending**

upon him: And there came a voice from heaven, saying,
Thou art my beloved Son, in whom I am well pleased.
And immediately the Spirit driveth him into the
wilderness. And he was there in the wilderness forty
days, tempted of Satan; and was with the wild beasts;
and the angels ministered unto him.

▶ Identity brings process, which brings the image of Christ
and preeminence:
**Matthew 4:1**

What did Christ defeat in the wilderness that we have to
manage?

*Giving thanks unto the Father, which hath made us meet
to be partakers of the inheritance of the saints in light:
Who hath delivered us from the power of darkness, and
hath translated us into the kingdom of his dear Son: In
whom we have redemption through his blood, even the
forgiveness of sins: Who is the image of the invisible God,
the firstborn of every creature: For by him were all things
created, that are in heaven, and that are in earth, visible
and invisible, whether they be thrones, or dominions, or
principalities, or powers: all things were created by him,
and for him: And he is before all things, and by him all
things consist. And he is the head of the body, the church:
who is the beginning, the firstborn from the dead; that in
all things he might have the preeminence.*
*Colossians 1:12-18*

Arts and Entertainment

Arts and Entertainment should reflect the glory and majesty
of our God. May we be instruments to celebrate His
creativity in the (1) arts, (2) music, (3) sports, (4) fashion,

(5) entertainment, and (6) every other way we celebrate and enjoy life.

There is nothing better for a man than to eat and drink and tell himself that his labor is good. This is from the hand of God. For who can eat and who can have enjoyment without Him? - Ecclesiastes 2.24

"Nevertheless I have a few things against you, because you allow that woman Jezebel, who calls herself a Prophetess, to teach and seduce my servants" (Revelation 2:20).

Moreover David and the captains of the army separated for the service some of the sons of Asaph . . . who should prophesy with harps, stringed instruments and cymbals (1 Chronicles 25:1).

And it came to pass when the priests came out of the Most Holy Place...and the Levites who were singers...stood at the east end of the altar, clothed in white linen, having cymbals, stringed instruments and harps, and with them one hundred and twenty priests sounding with trumpets- indeed it came to pass, when the trumpets and the singers were as one, to make one sound to be heard in praising and thanking the Lord, and when they lifted up their voice with trumpets and cymbals and instruments of music, and praised the Lord saying; For He is good, For His mercy endures forever, that the house, the house of the Lord, was filled with a cloud, so that the priests could not continue ministering because of the cloud; for the glory of the Lord filled the house of God (2 Chronicles 5:11-14).

Joshua and the Seven Enemies

**Then Joshua commanded the officers of the people, saying, "Pass through the camp and command the people, saying, 'Prepare provisions for yourselves, for within three days you will cross over this Jordan, to go in to possess the land which the Lord your God is giving you to possess." Joshua 1:10-11**

God wants us to have a mind of "having dominion" yet we are the ones that seem to be passive.

Business should be viewed as a place to worship God through the area of our calling. May we worship You through our gifts, talents and resources to build Your Kingdom. **"Remember the Lord your God, for it is He who gives you the ability to produce wealth" (Deuteronomy 8:18)**

**"No servant can serve two masters; for either he will hate the one and love the other, or else he will be loyal to one and despise the other. You cannot serve God and mammon" (Luke 16:13)**

**And whatever you do, do it heartily, as to the Lord and not to men, knowing that from the Lord you will receive the reward of the inheritance; for you serve the Lord Christ (Colossians 3:23-25)**

Jesus, Lord over all domains of influence (not just Lord over salvation)

> 1. King of Kings –Lord of Justice
> 2. Jehovah Jireh – Lord of Economics
> 3. Father - Lord of the Family

4. Creator God - Lord of Science and Technology
5. Living Word - Lord of Communication
6. Potter - Lord of the Arts and Beauty
7. Great Teacher - Lord of Education

Joshua and the Seven Enemies

Then Joshua commanded the officers of the people, saying, **"Pass through the camp and command the people, saying, 'Prepare provisions for yourselves, for within three days you will cross over this Jordan, to go in to possess the land which the Lord your God is giving you to possess.'"**
**Joshua 1:10-11**

Displace Seven Enemies (mountains) to take the Promised Land

**"This is how you will know that the living God is among you and that he will certainly drive out 7 enemies before you including the Canaanites, Hittites, Hivites, Perizzites, Girgashites, Amorites and the Jebusites"**
**(Joshua 3:10).**

Seven Nations Greater and Mightier

**"When the Lord your God brings you into the land which you go to possess, and has cast out many nations before you, the Hittites and the Girgashites and the Amorites and the Canaanites and the Perizzites and theHivites and the Jebusites, seven nations greater and mightier than thou" (Deuteronomy 7:1)** Yet God still says I have given you the land therefore go in and possess it.

## Seven Areas of Personal Influence

1) Jesus
2) Family
3) Work
4) Local Church
5) City/Community
6) Nation
7) World

## Education:

Words such as study, train--education should reflect the truth about God and man so that the truth shall make us free. May we seek and promote the true meaning of life through education.
The "fear of the Lord is the beginning of wisdom," and wisdom is the goal of education. There can be no true wisdom that does not begin with a proper "fear of the Lord."

**Say to wisdom, "You are my sister," and call understanding your kinsman. -Proverbs 7:4**

**Train up a child in the way that he should go, and when he is old he will not depart from it (Proverbs 22:6).**

**And I have filled him with the Spirit of God, in wisdom, in understanding, in knowledge, and in all manner of workmanship, to design artistic works, to work in gold, in silver, in bronze, in cutting jewels for setting, in carving wood, and to work in all manner of workmanship (Exodus 31:3-5).**

Teach me good judgment and knowledge, For I believe Your commandments (Psalm 119:66).

<u>Family:</u>

God formed them male and female in order to establish families to reflect His glory. May we restore Christ as the head of our families.

A father of the fatherless, a defender of widows, Is God in His holy habitation, God sets the solitary in families; He brings out those who are bound into prosperity (Psalm 68: 5-6).

Wives, submit to your own husbands, as to the Lord... Husbands, love your wives, as Christ loved the church and gave Himself up for her... Honor your father and mother... that it may go well with you and that you may live long in the land.-Ephesians 5:22, 25, 6:2,3

But know this that in the last days perilous times will come. For men will be lovers of themselves, lovers of money, boasters, proud, blasphemers, disobedient to parents, unthankful, unholy, unloving, unforgiving, slanderers, without self-control, brutal, despisers of good, traitors, headstrong, haughty, lovers of pleasure rather than lovers of God (2 Timothy 3:1-4).

"Behold, I will send you Elijah, the Prophet, before the great and dreadful day of the Lord, and he will turn the hearts of the fathers to the children, and the hearts of the children to their fathers, Lest, I come and strike the earth with a curse" (Malachi 4:5-6).

Government

God gave man government to establish freedoms and boundaries. May we reflect His loving-kindness and righteous judgments in our government.

**"For unto us a Child is born, unto us a Son is given; And the government will be upon His shoulder, and His name will be called Wonderful, Counselor, Mighty God, Everlasting Father, Prince of Peace. Of the increase of His government and peace there will be no end, upon the throne of David and over His kingdom, to order it and establish it with judgment and justice. From that time and forever the zeal of the Lord will perform this" (Isaiah 9:6-7).**

**"When the righteous are in authority, the people rejoice, but when a wicked man rules, the people groan" (Proverbs 29:2).**

**Let every soul be subject to the governing authorities. For there is no authority except from God, and the authorities that exist are appointed by God. Therefore whoever resists the authority resists the ordinance of God, and those who resist will bring judgment on themselves. For rulers are not a terror to good works, but to evil. Do you want to be unafraid of the authority? Do what is good, and you will have praise from the same. For he is God's minister to you for good. But if you do evil, be afraid; for he does not bear the sword in vain; for he is God's minister, an avenger to execute wrath on him who practices evil (Romans 13:1-4).**

<u>Media</u>

God communicated to man through a variety of ways. May we restore the ability to communicate truth and good news using His creative avenues.

**How beautiful on the mountains are the feet of those who bring good news, who proclaim peace, who bring good tidings, who proclaim salvation, who say to Zion, "Your God reigns!" (Isaiah 52:7)**

**As cold water to a weary soul, so is good news from a far country (Proverbs 25:25).**

**"The Spirit of the Lord is upon Me, because the Lord has anointed Me, to preach good tidings to the poor: He has sent Me to heal the brokenhearted, to proclaim liberty to the captives, and the opening of the prison to those who are bound" (Isaiah 61:1).**

**O, Zion, you who bring good tidings, get up, into the high mountains; O Jerusalem, you who bring good tidings, lift up your voice with strength (Isaiah 40:9).**

<u>Religion</u>

God never gave man a religion, but an opportunity for an intimate relationship with his Creator. May we come to know His presence and power in each of our lives.

**For God so loved the world that He gave His only begotten Son, that whoever believes in Him should not perish but have everlasting life. For God did not send**

His Son into the world to condemn the world, but that the world through Him might be saved. John 3:16-17

If any of you wants to be My follower, you must put aside your selfish ambition, shoulder your cross, and follow Me. -Matthew 16.24

Thus says the Lord: "Let not the wise man glory in his wisdom, Let not the mighty man glory in his might, Nor let the rich man glory in his riches; But let him who glories glory in this, That he understands and knows Me, That I am the Lord, exercising loving-kindness, judgment, and righteousness in the earth. For in these I delight," says the Lord. -- Jeremiah 9:23-24

Then he said to Him,"If Your Presence does not go with us, do not bring us up from here. For how then will it be known that Your people and I have found grace in Your sight, except You go with us? So we shall be separate, Your people and I, from all the people who are upon the face of the earth."-- Exodus 33:15-16

# The Mind Molders

## THE SEVEN MOUNTAIN PROPHECY BY JOHNNY ENLOW

| MOUNTAIN | ENEMY ON THE MOUNTAIN | PRINCIPALITY ON THE MOUNTAIN | SIGNIFICANT DISPLACING AUTHORITY | BASIC MISSION | REVELATION 5:12 KEY |
|---|---|---|---|---|---|
| MEDIA | Hittites (rep. bad news) | Apollyon (destroyer) | Evangelists | Fill the airwaves with "good news" | Blessing |
| GOVERNMENT | Girgashites (represent corruption) | Lucifer (pride and manipulation) | Apostles | Fill government positions with humble, servant leaders with integrity | Power |
| EDUCATION | Amorites (represent humanism) | Beelzebub (lies) | Teachers | Bring in new fear-of-God based curriculum | Wisdom |
| ECONOMY | Canaanites (represent love of money) | Mammon (greed) | Prophets | Discover and transfer wealth into kingdom purposes | Riches |
| CELEBRATION | Hivites (represents compromise) | Jezebel (seduction) | Prophets | Model the greater creative arts of God and prophesy through them | Glory |
| RELIGION | Perizzites (represent idolatry) | The religious spirit (false worship) | Holy Spirit | Model a Holy Spirit – infused life and ministry | Honour |
| FAMILY | Jebusites (represent rejection) | Baal (perversion) | Pastors | Impact social systems so that the family unit is prioritized | Strength |

## Chapter 7

# Conquering Your Battle Ground

### Understanding the Battle Ground

There are times that we go through things in our personal life, ministry or even on our jobs and we sometimes wonder if it is us, the devil or even God taking us through something to teach us. First of all God does not test or try us. The Bible says in the book of **James 1:15 "every man is tempted when he is drawn away of his own lust and enticed".**

I believe we have to start to understand what is God and what is not. Through many situations toil and snares we suffer challenges, yet we have to identify who is behind it all so we will know who to fight. Many times we fight each other because we think it is our brother, sister, husband or maybe even our wives. We think such things even though we know **Ephesians 6:12 "for we wrestle not against flesh and blood, but against principalities, against powers, against the rulers of the darkness of this world, against spiritual wickedness in high places."**

Most of us are not aware of our battle ground or where the attack is coming from. We have not been taught to do battle and no wonder we are clueless of where it's coming from. We have been trained to receive blessing, and all good things which is good, however we have to know that there is an enemy out there and, at one point or another, you will need to fight. Please be advised you will not always have to fight as in warfare, but sometimes it may the good fight, another time it may be a serious battle where you have to take something by force **"And from the days of John the Baptist until now the kingdom of heaven suffereth violence, and the violent take it by force". Matthew 11:12**

As a result, we have developed a welfare mentality and I believe God is preparing us to understand the battle ground where we win every time. Some of us that may have had particular experiences in God know something about fighting, therefore we have developed a mentality that everybody is after us which is just as bad as having a welfare mentality always expecting someone to give us something (anything). When we look at these two mindsets we realize that everybody is not against us and God is not some cosmic Santa Clause that is going to give us everything that we want regardless of whether we worked for it or not. At one point or another we need to get our believer working and believe for things, vs. having God to just hand us things all the time without us exercising our faith. Remember whatever kind of battle it may be, we will have to walk by faith.

God gave me the assignment of making sure that you and I are ready for the battle ground by way of understanding and prophetically declaring. God spoke to me about making sure that we understood the battle ground. God explained, there is a battle going on whether you and I understand it or not and you and I are literally the prize. God intends to win but He needs our cooperation to do so. We have not understood the battleground; therefore, Satan was able to lure us without us consciously knowing where we were going.

Some of you are in a battle right now and some of you have already fought some battles. Some of you feel like you won, some feel like you lost and some feel like you did not win or lose you were just engaged in a fight. One of the major reasons for our defeat is that we 1) did not understand the battle ground and 2) we have been lured on those grounds and, consequently, ended up looking like a defeated foe. We are not defeated foes, we simply did not understand what we were fighting for, why we were fighting or why we are even engaged in this battle.

Have you ever had some kind of a relationship (i.e. brother/sister, husband/wife etc.) and you constantly have the same kind of battles with them and you question "Why are we even having this battle?" You wonder "Why are we engaged in this conversation, we have known each other all this time and we are still right here?" What is going on with this? Why are we still at this place of conflict, still arguing about money, still arguing about bills and debt? We have already agreed to stay on our budget and to get out of debt. Why are we still arguing about why you keep spending and why I am so tight with the money? The answer is because we did not understand the battle ground. Any battle that you go into and you neglect to understand it must be repeated.

God gave me instructions about the battle ground. I know that you want me to tell you the battle ground is your mind (and maybe I will) but I am coming from a different perspective at this moment. Let me explain something about me. When I was a child and got into a conflict I knew that I could not fight so I would always take the first punch knowing I may not get another chance. Then I would run. At this point you'd have to catch me if you wanted to hit me back. I could not fight nor could I run well, however, it didn't matter how big you were because I was going to take the first swing. The devil does the same thing. You and I are wondering how the devil got that close to us and now we need to win the battle of our mind. He took the first swing and we left him an opening. How in the world did you and I get into so much trouble?

## Seduced By Our Enemy

We were seduced by an enemy that suckered us into a battle. The only thing that we have ever heard was that the mind (internal) was the battle ground. We have been taught for years that our mind was the battle ground and that is all we understood. Please understand that is one of the battle grounds, but before the enemy can get that close, you have to be seduced into coming close enough where he can even have access to your mind.

**Remember: "every man is tempted when he is drawn away and enticed." James 1:15**
When you are drawn away (not lead) you were seduced. Check out the meaning of the word seduce: *–verb (used with object),*

**1.** to lead astray, as from duty, rectitude, or the like; corrupt.
**2.** to persuade or induce to have sexual intercourse.
**3.** to lead or draw away, as from principles, faith, or allegiance: *He was seduced by the prospect of gain.*
**4.** to win over; attract; entice: *a supermarket seducing customers with special sales.*

This should give us an understanding of what has happened to us and how we went from peace to gradual chaos. I think by now you understand why I'm approaching the battle ground from these two perspectives:

1) The battle of position (External Battle)
2) The battle of the mind. (Internal Battle)

I want to take it from a different perspective. I want to talk about the external battle ground before I talk about the internal battle ground which is in our mind. The word of God tells us that we have peace. *John 14:27 Peace I leave with you, my peace I give unto you: not as the world giveth, give I unto you. Let not your heart be troubled, neither let it be afraid.* *KJV* Yet we know that a battle is going on and we are conscious of the battle. How can you have peace in a battle? It is possible! I don't know about you but I have been through some battles. I don't think that you can tell me about a battle that I have not been through. I have been through some of the best battles. I can't think of any battle where the devil has not been trying to (1) count us out and (2) shut us down. The only way that he can do that is to get inside of us because the only way to shut down the plant is to get inside the plant. Please know the devil does not start inside you. He has no access to you from the inside because God has taken residence in you and me. That is the reason for his spirit of seduction. Remember, there is a progression in the battle ground.

Progression One: **Regression**
Progression Two: **Suppression**
Progression Three: **Depression**
Progression Four: **Oppression**
Progression Five: **Obsession**
Progression Six: **Possession**

This external battle is designed by the enemy to gain access to the inside where he can control you and his altimeter goal is to gain control over your will which is the strongest force in the earth.

## The Internal Battle Ground

We need to understand these battle grounds. There is an external battle ground that the enemy has summoned us to. Now I know that this has never happened to any of you but the only time that I felt intimidated was when I ran into somebody else's house to fight. This only happened when the person hit me first. I thought "It's not going down like this; he used my game plan and ran". At the time I had a moment of insanity because I ran after him. When he went into his house I pursued him. When I arrived in his house his process changed and he felt that he was in safety. That was not the case, because I immediately tackled him and beat him up on the floor of his house. I felt intimidated, however, because his brothers and sisters were in the house and his mother was sitting on the sofa. When I came to myself I realized the trouble that I was in because none of my folks were around. When I elected to run into what I did not know would become a battle ground, I did feel intimidated but intimidation did not hit beforehand.

That is what the devil does; he lures us into his battle ground and defeats us every time. He is supposed to because it is his battle ground and God never told us to go there. That battle ground was selected by the devil and we ran after it or into it and many times to our demise.

Remember, God has planned no defeat for you and me; we are "more than Conquerors through Christ Jesus". Then why do we feel defeated? We closed the door on what happened to us and we made that the end. When that person hit me and I took the hit what if I had called that the end? A moment of insanity refused to let me call that the end. What is it that you are calling the end when God never intended for that to be the end. You accepted that as defeat when God never considered that the end. What if God would have called Adam's defeat the end then there would have never been grace for you and me.

My assignment is to prepare you for a battle ground. If given access to your battle ground the enemy tries to stagnate, paralyze and to shut you down. Your battle ground is your battle ground. We think that the enemy can just show up when he wants to but we have to give him access. When we really understand your battle ground is not somewhere the enemy can just show up, we give him access when we leave a door open for him to choose the battle ground. If you recall when there was going to be a (physical) fight, you and I would choose where the battle ground was going to be. Remember what we use to do as children? We would say to our opponent meet me behind the school at 3 o'clock. At that point we have chosen the battle ground. It is always a mistake for you to choose the battle ground and I show up, but that is what we do. The Devil selects the battle ground and when you and I show up, that is an automatic defeat. With all the power of God that is on us, when we let the Devil select the battleground, it is an automatic defeat.

God has planned no defeat for us. This might be a tremendous revelation for us because we are trying to figure out why is it that we have obeyed God and been defeated. Any defeat that is planned for you is a judgment against you. God did not plan your defeat. Now we want to question what happened. How did we obey God and still become defeated? One of the things that you should know and remember is that faith without obedience does not manifest victory in your life. That means that if you and I call ourselves having faith regarding something and we are not in step with obedience then that does not manifest any victory. Literality what has happened is that the Devil has called you on a battle ground and you were the victim. Why? Because you did not hear God say come to this ground. You were not led by the Spirit of God to come to this ground. You were following the enemy on the ground and there was no victory for you.

The best place in the Bible that we can go to see this is Jesus in the wilderness in Matthew chapter 4. He was led up into the wilderness by the Spirit; this is a capitol S indicating that He was led up into the wilderness by the Holy Spirit to be tempted of the Devil (*Matthew 4:1 Then was Jesus led up of the Spirit into the wilderness to be tempted of the devil). KJV* God selected Jesus' battle ground, the devil showed up. Most of us are going to a place where the devil has selected the battle ground but God had selected the battle ground for Jesus and the devil has come to the battle ground that that God had already selected as the ground.

The tempter is not always present. We see that in *Matthew 4:3 And when the tempter came to him, he said, If thou be the Son of God, command that these stones be made bread. KJV*. A lot of times we think that we have experienced complete victory but what has actually happened is that the tempter has not come yet. Now when the tempter come to Jesus the tempter "said" – the temper uses words, he is trying to reach your mind. The tempter does not have any access at this point because Jesus has not given him any. At this point he only has an **external** battle ground. The ground that the tempter really wants to conquer is your **internal** battle ground. Your battle is not an external battle ground and you cannot give him access to your battle ground, because it is an **internal** battle ground. However, we are always giving him access to our battle ground; he cannot get access unless we give it to him. Remember, there is an **external** battle ground and there is an **internal** battle ground and with this external battle ground you can win every time.

If God ever tells you or leads you into a battle you have already won. The devil is the defeated one. Assess the battle that you are going through now. If you are having a battle in your mind you have already let the devil go too far. He is <u>not</u> supposed to get that far. You have already been lured to the battle ground that the tempter has selected. If you are in the battle ground that God has selected, the tempter has to come because he is not there when you get there.

Remember, when I talked about meeting another child behind the school at 3. I chose the battle ground. God is trying to educate us in the battle ground to keep you in charge of the battle. He wants to win, however, He is not going to win if you cave in and quit. God wants us to win every time. God wants us to keep a peace of mind in the battle. When God chooses the battle ground you may not see how it is going to work but you just stand on the fact that God <u>said</u> and keep standing on that.

My daughter had a situation that caused me to start to imagine what she was going through. One of the items was a hospital bill of over $600,000.00. She went on and on talking about the bill and other associated matters. At first I tried to imagine what she was saying, but I had to shut that down because I cannot afford to imagine anything that is raising itself above the knowledge of God. When you are on the battle ground, don't imagine, especially if you are trying to help someone else fight. She did not choose for those things to happen to her and I did not have any answers at first, however, so much good came out of that bad situation it could not possibly solely been the devil. This is what I finally said "you will not have to pay that bill". I did not have any basis to say that except the Spirit of God revealed it to me. I am seeing the devil being defeated over and over again in her situation and I decided that I will not be moved by circumstances because God <u>said</u>. Now since God gave me that word I am going to remain sensitive to the rest of what God is saying so we know what to do. The bottom line is she did not have to pay it. The government did not have to pay. The ones that were responsible for it paid. She took advantage of everything that they offered because this was God defending her.

When the devil calls you on a ground and you don't show up, God will show up and God will make them pay double. When you are in that kind of position you have to be quiet. Since you are not conscious of the battle ground and you don't know what to say, DON'T SAY ANYTHING. Just say to God "I know you see this" and trust God and you can win every battle.

You winning every battle is not unattainable. Jesus won every battle but the one He surrendered. Jesus said no one takes my life, I give it up. He said this in *John 10:18 No man taketh it from me, but I lay it down of myself. I have power to lay it down, and I have power to take it again. This commandment have I received of my Father.* Remember, when they came to arrest Him and he asked them "Whom seek ye?" They said Jesus of Nazareth. Jesus had eleven of His disciples with him, only Judas was missing. When he answered them saying "I am He", they all fell to the ground. We find the account of this in *John 18:4-6, 4 Jesus therefore, knowing all things that should come upon him, went forth, and said unto them, Whom seek ye? 5 They answered him, Jesus of Nazareth. Jesus saith unto them, I am he. And Judas also, which betrayed him, stood with them. 6 As soon then as he had said unto them, I am he, they went backward, and fell to the ground.* He did not put His hands on anyone, He just said "I am He" and they fell out under the power of God. He then waits for them to come back to themselves and said in *John 18:8 8 Jesus answered, I have told you that I am he: if therefore ye seek me, let these go their way: KJV* Jesus asked them to let the eleven go and to take Him and they did, but the truth of the matter is that they did not take Him, He went with them willingly. He could have said the same thing and released the same power and got away but He understood that it was time now. What time was He talking about? He understood that it was time for Him to go to the devils battleground. He went to the place where it was already clear that He would be slaughtered there. He allowed them to take Him, He allowed them to beat Him, He allowed them to do it all because at any given moment He could have asked for more than 12 legions of angels to come and get him and they would have showed up so the battle was always His even at that place of Calvary. He could have won the battle even then but He **voluntarily** became the sacrifice.

I do not want to hurt your feeling or damage your religion but I want you to understand that you choose the battle ground. You and I wear a cross but we don't know the meaning of it. It is not a holy symbol, but it is a symbol that represents the place where He gave His life. It's a symbol that represents what happened but you and I embrace it as a holy symbol. The Star of David was a holy symbol--the cross is not, no more than the serpent in the wilderness was a holy symbol; it merely represented Christ. This is something that we must understand or we will be defeated in our battle ground. A bad perception of a great reality is not any good. When we go into a battle and have a bad perception of a great reality it is not any good. We don't know why we are there and as a result we do not understand our battle ground. We, therefore, minimize that whole experience. When we have a moment in the battle ground we have to understand that we have come to win and we must come to rely on the grace of God. We don't come to rely on the grace of God as if we can go ahead and lay down in sin because God will forgive me – not in the battle ground. If we do, we are about to be defeated in the battle ground. We do rely on the grace of God to empower us to defeat the devil at this point. We show up on the battle ground as a victor in the battle ground.

The battle ground has been selected by God. You stepped into that battle ground because that is the ground where God wanted His grace to show up so that you could defeat your enemy there. Here is the problem; we rely on the wrong grace in the right place. There is a grace that empowers, that is the grace for grown up folks, that is the grace for those who are grown up in God because they know how to sling their Word, handle their shield and where to put their helmet.

Does this mean that you throw away the grace that pardons us of the sin that we committed? No, we don't throw that away. It has its proper place but that place is not on the battle ground.

In *2 Corinthians 10:3-5 For though we walk in the flesh, we do not war after the flesh: (For the weapons of our warfare are not carnal, but mighty through God to the pulling down of strong holds;) Casting down imaginations, and every high thing that exalteth itself against the knowledge of God, and bringing into captivity every thought to the obedience of Christ; KJV* We see in verse 5 the casting down of imaginations, remember the imagination is in the mind and that is your internal battle ground. So when the enemy speaks words to you, he speaks to gain access to your battle ground which is your thought realm. Some of us are already seduced to come this particular battle ground. We followed the bait to come to this battle ground. Check this out in Philippians *2:5-10 Let this mind be in you, which was also in Christ Jesus: Who, being in the form of God, thought it not robbery to be equal with God: But made himself of no reputation, and took upon him the form of a servant, and was made in the likeness of men: And being found in fashion as a man, he humbled himself, and became obedient unto death, even the death of the cross. Wherefore God also hath highly exalted him, and given him a name which is above every name: That at the name of Jesus every knee should bow, of things in heaven, and things in earth, and things under the earth; KJV* We need the mind of Christ Jesus, but some of us have already been drawn away by our on lust so that we can be slaughtered in this particular battle ground.

One of the things that we have to do is to overcome this is to get delivered from people. God spoke to me regarding this in my private prayer time and I found myself repenting. I came to the understanding that I have nothing to prove to any man. Many of us battle with this because we feel that we have to prove this or that to somebody and that is the seduction. We want to become a star because we have something to prove. We want mega money because we have something to prove. We are putting on a show for husbands, wives, Bishops, Pastors and people in our circle of influence because we have something to prove. We want to be on television because we have something to prove. We want to own things because we have something to prove. But we have nothing to prove and I hit that reality in my prayer time. I have nothing to prove to anyone. My soul purpose for being in the earth is to bring glory to God, my Father in heaven.

You and I have danced the dance and sang the song trying to prove something to somebody. We have one thing to prove and that is to God alone. We have to realize that God alone is great. Our assignment is to tear the works of the devil down and in doing so our Father will be glorified. God does not like attention getters. We have one purpose and one purpose alone. At my church we are about to change some things, we are no longer having any services to prove something to somebody, God can move whenever He wants for as long as He wants and if it is too long for anybody they can leave and come back next week. This does not mean that we will hold up the program with flesh. It means as long as God is moving we will step out of the way and let Him move and we have to know the difference. When you and I are putting on a show for somebody, God does not like it because He will not share His glory with anybody. We have to make sure that everything that we do and every breath that we breathe glorifies God. Too many of us have already fallen for the bait and we must settle this today.

Do you realize how many men, and even Holy Ghost pimps, try to see how many women they can get just because they feel that they have something to prove to somebody? God says I am not glorified in that because our sole purpose is to bring Him Glory. Remember *Philippians 2:5-10 Let this mind be in you, which was also in Christ Jesus: Who, being in the form of God, thought it not robbery to be equal with God: But made himself of no reputation, and took upon him the form of a servant, and was made in the likeness of men.* In verse 7, He made Himself of no reputation, but we have major battles trying to prove to someone in the earth that we are great. But how does God see us? Jesus stepped down out of a holy heaven and took upon Him the form of a servant and made of Himself no reputation but He became the greatest reputation in the earth. He would heal the sick and say don't tell anybody. But we heal the sick and say look what I did, but we did not do it, it was Jesus working with us confirming the word with signs and wonders. You and I did nothing but obeyed the leading of the Lord.

We live in a different reality and the only real stars are the ones that God makes, not the one we make ourselves. We have to desire to glorify God. My former pastor, Apostle Betty Peebles, went home to be with the Lord recently and she coined the phrase "Performing for an audience of One". I was not around when she coined this phrase but I saw it and it blessed me. Think about that. How many people are you performing for? It has been written concerning her that she has done what no other woman on the planet has done performing for an audience of one. If we look at the life of Jesus we will see that He lived what she put into words. Jesus was performing for an audience of one, His Father God. Jesus would say all of the time "I came to do the will of my Father or I say only what I hear Him say" He was performing for an audience of one. Jesus says in John *6:38 For I came down from heaven, not to do mine own will, but the will of him that sent me. KJV* He was performing for an audience of one.

Three things about the battle ground that you should know and remember:

1. The battle ground should always be the place that God chooses.
2. You should be led by the Holy Spirit into that place.
3. The tempter had to come to the place that God has chosen.

If you understand that you will have victory. God will lead you into your wealthy place.

I have chosen another place in the bible for you to see that God chooses the battle ground. This is found in Numbers chapter 16. The scenario is that Korah has come against Moses and had chosen some choice leaders to join him in doing so. Moses is in a battle now because he realizes that people that he thought were with him were not with him. Their thought was that Moses took too much upon himself. They wanted to know "why do you see yourself bigger than us?" God talks to us too!

*Numbers 16:15-36 - And Moses was very wroth, and said unto the LORD, Respect not thou their offering:* Moses was trying to get them into their wealthy place but now Moses is saying not to respect their offering, this is one of the reasons that I do not put my mouth on men or women of God because they can say this any time "don't respect his offering" notice that Moses says to God that he is not guilty of anything. *I have not taken one ass from them, neither have I hurt one of them. And Moses said unto Korah, Be thou and all thy company before the LORD, thou, and they, and Aaron, tomorrow*: this is the place where Moses selected the battle ground. Korah is wrong and he is letting Moses select a battle ground in the presence of God. This is an absolute defeat in this situation. Moses named the place and the time.

You must do the same; name the place and the time. *And take every man his censer, and put incense in them, and bring ye before the LORD every man his censer, two hundred and fifty censers; thou also, and Aaron, each of you his censer. And they took every man his censer, and put fire in them, and laid incense thereon, and stood in the door of the tabernacle of the congregation with Moses and Aaron. And Korah gathered all the congregation against them unto the door of the tabernacle of the congregation:* the door of the tabernacle was the place of the battle ground, now Moses has said where to come, when to come and what time to come. Korah was expecting to win but he was wrong he was going to be defeated *and the glory of the LORD appeared unto all the congregation.* God's glory appeared, there is a back side of the hand of God and a front side of the hand of God and you have to decide which side you want. The front side holds blessing. Which side do you want? You choose the side you want by your actions. Some of us are getting the back side of the hand of God because of our actions. We chose to fight on a battle ground that God never told us to go to. You are having this battle and you lost. Most of the time when we have determined that the battle was over, it was not. Most of the time when I have marked the battle as being over it was not, because God had not determined that it was over. Remember God sets the battle. But take a look at Korah's defeat in the rest of this passage. *And the LORD spake unto Moses and unto Aaron, saying, Separate yourselves from among this congregation, that I may consume them in a moment. And they fell upon their faces, and said, O God, the God of the spirits of all flesh, shall one man sin, and wilt thou be wroth with all the congregation? And the LORD spake unto Moses, saying, Speak unto the congregation, saying, Get you up from about the tabernacle of Korah, Dathan, and Abiram. And Moses rose up and went unto Dathan and Abiram; and the elders of Israel followed him. And he spake unto the congregation, saying, Depart, I pray you, from the tents of these wicked men, and touch nothing of theirs, lest ye be consumed in all their sins. So they got up from the tabernacle of Korah, Dathan, and Abiram, on every side: and Dathan and Abiram came out, and stood in the door of their tents, and their wives, and their sons, and their little children. And Moses said, Hereby ye shall know that the LORD hath sent me to do all these works; for I have not done them of mine own mind. If these men die the common death of all men, or if they be visited after the visitation of all men; then the LORD hath not sent me. But if the LORD make a new thing, and the earth open her mouth, and swallow them up, with all that appertain unto them, and they go down quick into the pit; then ye shall understand that these men have provoked the LORD. And it came to pass, as he had made an end of speaking all these words, that the ground clave asunder that was under them: And the earth opened her mouth, and swallowed them up, and their houses, and all the men that appertained unto Korah, and all their goods. They, and all that appertained to them, went down alive into the pit, and the earth closed upon them: and they perished from among the congregation. And all Israel that were round about them fled at the cry of them: for they said, Lest the earth swallow us up also. And there came out a fire from the LORD, and consumed the two hundred and fifty men that offered incense. KJV*

You and I have to have the right mindset; God has already set us up as winners. Many of us are going into battle but we don't have the right mindset. Have you ever watched karate or boxing movies? You may have been focused on the fight, the fight is the battle, but the best part is the mentoring. One pattern that they have in common is to never lose your temper or you will lose the fight. When you become angry you do things to hurt yourself.

One of the things that people do when they get angry is to go out and spend money that they should not spend and they think that the devil is really going to be mad, however, the truth is that you only hurt yourself. Now you can't pay your mortgage or your rent, you can't pay utility bills, etc. Who did you hurt? Certainly not the devil. I have looked at many professional fights and the moment that an opponent lost their temper is the moment they begin to lose the fight. Your temper is attached to your emotions. Never allow anyone to make you angry because when that happens you have loss control of the battle.

Let's go to another place where we can see what I am talking about *2 Corinthians 10:3-5 For though we walk in the flesh, we do not war after the flesh:* why do we try to win with natural things? This is a spiritual battle and if you are in the battle God should have called it. *4(For the weapons of our warfare are not carnal, but mighty through God to the pulling down of strong holds;)* We can see from this verse that God calls the battle. You have to walk away from some things even if you think that they may call you a punk. You may think that you won the victory because you get a natural victory but you are not in a natural battle you are in a spiritual battle, so who really won? What is a strong hold? It is the place where the devil lures you into a battle at the place he chose. *Casting down imaginations,* The imagination is in the mind and that is an internal battle ground. Verse 5 says cast that down *and every high thing that exalteth itself against the knowledge of God, and bringing into captivity every thought to the obedience of Christ; KJV.* Remember you have go to the battle ground that God chooses which is external and not the one the devil wants to lure you to which is internal. Remember my story about how I fought as a child. I would choose the battle with words – we called those words selling wolf tickets, which means I could not back up my words. I did not know that this was the way God did it. I won the battle with words most of the time and they did not know that I could not fight. David understood this principle; he used words to select the battle ground that God had chosen when he was going to fight Goliath, we see that in *1 Samuel 17:37 37 David said moreover, The LORD that delivered me out of the paw of the lion, and out of the paw of the bear, he will deliver me out of the hand of this Philistine. And Saul said unto David, Go, and the LORD be with thee. KJV* You can do the same thing, you can say "God is going to deliver me from this just like He did from the last thing that I battled with, God wants me to win against tumors, cancer, financial distress, legal matters and any other thing that exalts itself against the knowledge of God and bring that into the obedience of Christ. These things that I am facing now will be as one of those things that God has already delivered me from. God wants me to win."

David comes out with no armor on ready for battle. One of the first things that he said was "who is this uncircumcised Philistine that he should defy the armies of the living God' *1 Sam 17:26, And David spake to the men that stood by him, saying, What shall be done to the man that killeth this Philistine, and taketh away the reproach from Israel? for who is this uncircumcised Philistine, that he should defy the armies of the living God? KJV* David said that this uncircumcised Philistine will be like the bear and the lion. Are we not the army of the living God? We have to have the correct mindset and understand covenant, we have a covenant with the most high God.

My wife and I were praying and I became overwhelmed by the presence of God and I began to say "To you be the glory, God". In this battle ground you and I have to understand that it is Him. I became overwhelmed in His presence and I understood what He was impressing upon me from *Philippians 2:5-7 Let this mind be in you, which was also in Christ Jesus: Who, being in the form of God, thought it not robbery to be equal with God: But made himself of no reputation, and took upon him the form of a servant, and was made in the likeness of men: KJV* Jesus made Himself of no reputation. I understood that you and I have nothing to prove to anybody. We have spent so much time trying to prove something to this person or that person but we do not need to prove anything to anyone. People become ashamed because they are trying to prove things to people and when we do that we end up disapproving God. God want us just to be ourselves not try to prove anything to anybody. We should not try to prove anything to anybody whether we pray, preach, sing etc. When we don't have anything to prove to anybody then God gets the glory. To God be the glory for whatever we do. If we make a mistake or say something wrong we may become bashful and ashamed and that is because we want to prove something. If you are a singer or musician and miss a note, so what, just keep on going. Most of us won't know anyway if you don't have anything to prove to anyone.

I put pressure on me to take care of some things that I want to change in my life, and I struggled when I was trying to prove it to someone. When I decided to do it for me I was able to make the change that I wanted. It never happened when I was doing it to prove something to other people. If you have ever done this then let me set you free as far as I am concerned. You don't have to do one single thing to win my approval. You have my approval. You do not do things to get approval. Be who you are! The best person you can ever be is who you are there is absolutely nothing wrong with you. You are a unique person and God wants to use your uniqueness just the way you are.

**Preparation For Your Battle Ground**

I believe that we can live a life of victory, remember it is possible for you to obey God and lose battles. I want to focus on four (4) principles that prepare you to win battles. Anything that the enemy brings against us we can actually win every time. I believe that one of the most exciting things that we can do is to actually win the attacks that the devil brings against us. You may be one of those that desired to do some things and you know that you did not win because of the devil. This information is going to help you tremendously. One of the things that will help tremendously as we embrace the four principles that cause us to win the battle every time is a lifestyle of prayer. God keeps pushing us until we have a lifestyle of prayer. Not just the hour a day or every other day but a lifestyle of talking to God. God has more to say that we could imagine. Some people don't think that God has that much to say and those may be the ones that talk a lot, they talk to hear themselves talk, or to impress themselves. God only talks so that He can get information to us so that we can hear what He wants us to do and what He wants us to know.

As we look at understanding the battle ground, the first thing that we have to do is to recognize what Jesus did. In Matthew chapter 4 we see that Jesus was designed to come into a level of temptation. This is a battle ground that God chose and it was a battle that Jesus was going to win. Sometimes we stumble into a battle ground and we are not armed or prepared to fight. Every one of us in the body of Christ is going to have a battle and if we have already been through a battle, the next one is intensified. We should not be surprised at what is going on. Jesus was led into the wilderness but He did not plan to stay there. He planned to beat the devil and come back out of the wilderness and that is what we should be doing; Going into the wilderness, planning to be victorious over the devil and coming back out. Some of us go into the wilderness as if we plan to stay there.

The four principles that Jesus employed to position Himself to win ever battle are as follows:

1. He submitted himself to spiritual authority.
2. He committed to fulfill all righteousness.
3. He walked under an open heaven.
4. He received the Spirit of God and walked in the light

These four principles were a series of things that happened before He was led by the Spirit of God into the wilderness to be tempted as described in Matthew chapter 4 verse one. All of these principles are seen right here in *Matthew 3:13-17 Then cometh Jesus from Galilee to Jordan unto John, to be baptized of him. 14 But John forbad him, saying, I have need to be baptized of thee, and comest thou to me? And Jesus answering said unto him, Suffer it to be so now: for thus it becometh us to fulfill all righteousness. Then he suffered him. And Jesus, when he was baptized, went up straightway out of the water: and, lo, the heavens were opened unto him, and he saw the Spirit of God descending like a dove, and lighting upon him: And lo a voice from heaven, saying, This is my beloved Son, in whom I am well pleased. KJV*

Here we are, the people of God, and we are not seeing the level of victory that God wants to see in our lives. How can that be possible? It is possible. In life there are going to be some battles but when they come up we have to win. Winning is a decision, you don't win by chance. You have purpose in your heart that you are going to win this one and you have to do what you are supposed to be doing in order to win. Jesus is our chief example setter and He won in every area of His life. He was tempted in all points just like you and I but He won at His battles. He did not quit when it was time to produce. We can't cave in, faint and quit, this is happening to people every day but it is not supposed to happen to us. We are not supposed to lose—that is to say, the body of Christ. If we obey what Jesus said and did we will have victory every time. Every time a battle came up Jesus was already set in position to win. That is the challenge with you and I, we are not already set in position to win. Now when the battle comes up we don't win because we were not in position to win. When I really understood this, it was only at that point that I started to win.

Let us look at what Jesus did in *Matthew 4:1-4 Then was Jesus led up of the Spirit into the wilderness to be tempted of the devil. And when he had fasted forty days and forty nights, he was afterward an hungered. And when the tempter came to him, he said, If thou be the Son of God, command that these stones be made bread. But he answered and said, It is written, Man shall not live by bread alone, but by every word that proceedeth out of the mouth of God. KJV* If we are going to win we have to live by every word that proceedeth out of the mouth of God and that is going to take commitment. How do you position yourself? If we are going to live by every word that proceedeth out the mouth of God we have to understand that is not a set place. Living by every word that proceedeth out of the mouth of God is something that is going to have to happen every day, but that is not what sets you. That is your action according to the position that you are set in. Let me give you an example of being in the right position.

Isn't it amazing that many of us want to be blessed financially but we don't do the things that positions us to be blessed financially. What position do you have to be in to be blessed financially? You must be employed, if you are not, you are not in position to be blessed financially. Another example: Maybe you want to save some money for something but do you have a bank account? If not, you are not in position to save money. You can't have a mindset to wait until you get employed to get a bank account because that is what puts you in position to save. Get $5 and open an account, use the money you were going to spend on fast food and when you do that three times you now have $15 and you are not even working. Another example: You want to have a good marriage, but you are always spending time with the boys or the girls and they are single. You are not in position to have a good marriage, because a single person cannot tell you how to stay married.

According to **Matthew 4:1** Jesus is led up of the Spirit into the wilderness. The first word of this verse is then. When the word "then" is used it means that something came before or something happened before Jesus was led up. Now what we have to do is go back and find out what the "then" is there for. We know chapter four (4) is about the battle. Jesus was in the wilderness fasting and praying and He did not necessarily think about being tested of the devil. I don't think that any of us have that in mind when we are approaching our testing and certainly not our time of being tempted of the devil. I know that I did not have that in mind as I was going through my test. When you went into that test you did not know what it was for. One of the things that amaze me is that some people decide to get married that are not prepared for the test. They only address the sweet part; you are the apple of my eye etc. and then later they wonder "is this what I signed up for?" The second you get married you are in position for there to be a battle even if you are not in position for the battle. If you are position properly you can keep the happiness even in the mist of the battle. Remember in **Matthew 4:1** Jesus was happy to go into the wilderness. When you are making all of the preparation the tempter is not present. Then when you are ready the tempter shows up and many of us are surprised. Many of us want ministry but we do not want the process. Many of us are in business but we don't want the process. Without the process we are not positioned. I remember one time there was a man that wanted to go into the restaurant business and someone suggested that he go and work for one, and when he did that he did not want to own a restaurant. He just wanted to cook for one because he did not want the process. He did not want the planning, the scheduling, the marketing, the supply issues and the customers that want a free meal.

Anything that you are not positioned for will shut you down mentally and that will cause you to lose the battle. Remember, we are talking about the external battle and the internal battle, the devil attacks us in the internal battle ground and that is the battle ground that he has prepared. If we are positioned according to the external battle ground that God has prepared, he will never be able to get to our internal battle ground (our mind) He cannot get to the internal battle ground until he shuts you down in the external and if you are not positioned for the battle, that's exactly what will happen. The number one mistake that we make is losing external battle and allowing the devil access to our mind. Remember, in *2 Kings 6:15-17 And when the servant of the man of God was risen early, and gone forth, behold, an host compassed the city both with horses and chariots.* Elisha was positioned for the battle but his servant was not so he said, *And his servant said unto him, Alas, my master! how shall we do? And the Prophets respond, he answered, Fear not: for they that be with us are more than they that be with them. And Elisha prayed, and said, LORD, I pray thee, open his eyes, that he may see. And the LORD opened the eyes of the young man; and he saw: and, behold, the mountain was full of horses and chariots of fire round about Elisha. KJV* The servant was affected by his mental and spiritual shutdown-- he was not positioned. The Prophet asked God to open his eyes and let him see. What happened at this moment was that the Prophet, that was the spiritual authority over his life, spoke and he was able to see. No matter what you are going through there is more with you than with them. God has already arranged victory for you so no matter what the enemy has planned. All you have to do is position yourself for the battle.

This concept can also be seen when Jehoshaphat was in battle, the battle was already set against him and he did not know what to do so he had to ask God. Have you ever been already in the battle and did not know what to do; well I have. I could not run nor could I go forward and all I could do was to pray. Jehoshaphat knew that he could not run, and that's what we have to do also; don't run but do what Jehoshaphat did in *2 Chronicles 20:13-15 And all Judah stood before the LORD, with their little ones, their wives, and their children. Then upon Jahaziel the son of Zechariah, the son of Benaiah, the son of Jeiel, the son of Mattaniah, a Levite of the sons of Asaph, came the Spirit of the LORD in the midst of the congregation; And he said, Hearken ye, all Judah, and ye inhabitants of Jerusalem, and thou king Jehoshaphat, Thus saith the LORD unto you, Be not afraid nor dismayed by reason of this great multitude; for the battle is not yours, but God's. KJV.* The word from God did not even come to Jehoshaphat but to one in the congregation saying that you shall not have to fight in this battle. God has established that this is a battle and now he begins to position Jehoshaphat for the battle but he has to listen to what God is saying to Jehoshaphat through Jahaziel in *2 Chronicles 20:16-18 Tomorrow go ye down against them: behold, they come up by the cliff of Ziz; and ye shall find them at the end of the brook, before the wilderness of Jeruel. Ye shall not need to fight in this battle: set yourselves, stand ye still, and see the salvation of the LORD with you, O Judah and Jerusalem: fear not, nor be dismayed; tomorrow go out against them: for the LORD will be with you. And Jehoshaphat bowed his head with his face to the ground: and all Judah and the inhabitants of Jerusalem fell before the LORD, worshipping the LORD. KJV* God told them to "set yourselves", "stand ye still" and "see the salvation of the LORD." What happens when the devil attacks you in the pre attack arena? He does this so that he can gain access to your thought world to shut you down spiritually, shut you down mentally and have you to be an emotional wreck. Now you can't think or hear God so what do you do? There is nothing that you can do except be beat by the devil.

Can you bounce back? Yes you can. Look what Jesus did in *Matthew 3:13-17 Then cometh Jesus from Galilee to Jordan unto John, to be baptized of him. 14 But John forbad him, saying, I have need to be baptized of thee, and comest thou to me? And Jesus answering said unto him, Suffer it to be so now: for thus it becometh us to fulfill all righteousness. Then he suffered him. And Jesus, when he was baptized , went up straightway out of the water: and, lo, the heavens were opened unto him, and he saw the Spirit of God descending like a dove, and lighting upon him: And lo a voice from heaven, saying, This is my beloved Son, in whom I am well pleased. KJV* Jesus did four things that positioned Him for the battle. Remember, I mentioned this earlier you are vulnerable to anyone that baptizes you. It only takes a few minutes for a person to drown. Baptizing is a risky business for pastors. I remember one occasion when I was helping a pastor baptize a 600 pound person. The baptismal pool was very small and it was old. The water was very cold because the pool was not heated and we were all cramped in that small pool. The pastor and I were totally responsible to get him under the water and back up again. The gentleman totally trusted us to take care of him. I remember thinking about that 600 pounds and realizing that we must get him down and up again because if we drop him he could drown. This gentleman was at our mercy just like Jesus was at the mercy of John.

Jesus put Himself at the mercy of John, His spiritual authority in the earth. John was the forerunner of Jesus and this is another way of saying that Jesus is the Successor of John. If I am training someone because they are to take my place then I am their forerunner. We can look at this and actually see that when John was getting ready to be beheaded he wanted to know that Jesus was actually in place. We see that in *Matthew 11:2-3 Now when John had heard in the prison the works of Christ, he sent two of his disciples, And said unto him, Art thou he that should come, or do we look for another? KJV* John sent his disciples to Jesus because he needed to know if Jesus was the one. John knew that he was about to be beheaded and he wanted to make sure because he knew that the ones that were planning to behead him did not give him life and they cannot take it away. If Jesus is the one that is to take his place and Jesus is actually in place, John knew that everything that was happening was okay.
Remember that John's disciples followed Jesus after John left

You cannot start ministry until get to this point of submitting to spiritual authority. Now let's revisit what Jesus did to position Himself to win the battle. The tragedy is that the ones that are in line to be announced as John did Jesus do not demonstrate any movement that resembles being ready to take the place of the spiritual authority. Some of the leaders in our church are called to the same battles that I am called to and more than likely by the time they get to a battle ground I have already left. But some of them have not even been to my training yet that end up at the battle ground. That means that they are not prepared for the battle ground. We have to be positioned properly in order to win the battle. Remember we talked earlier about the four principles that will ensure that you win the battle every time as you implement them in your life.

They are as follows:

(1). **He submitted himself to spiritual authority.** John was the one that was to introduce Jesus. John was here before Jesus and John was the spiritual authority that Jesus had to check in with and submit to because it was John's assignment to introduce Jesus. John had Jesus' file and he had authority to baptize him. The very first thing that Jesus was to submit himself under was the hand of John and it was only after this event that Jesus actually started his ministry. Who has been given your file? Who has the authority to release you into ministry? Somebody knows exactly what your next move ought to be. Remember, the sons of Issachar mentioned in *1 Chronicles 12:32 32 And of the children of Issachar, which were men that had understanding of the times, to know what Israel ought to do;....KJV When* the king has a problem and needed information they always went to the Prophet to hear a Prophetic word or they went to fortune tellers to consult with demons.

(2) **Commit to fulfill all righteousness.** When Jesus went to John to be baptized, John recognized a baptism that Jesus was designed to bring forth in *Matthew 3:11 I indeed baptize you*

*with water unto repentance: but he that cometh after me is mightier than I, whose shoes I am not worthy to bear: he shall baptize you with the Holy Ghost, and with fire: KJV* John wanted that baptism of fire that Jesus was going to introduce and John said I need to be baptized of you. Jesus answered and said *"Suffer it to be so now: for thus it becometh us to fulfill all righteousness. Then he suffered him".* Jesus was bringing in the baptism of fire and the baptism of fire does not come first. So they both agreed to commit to fulfill all righteousness. That should be true for you and me; anything that God is for, it is our position to fulfill it. Many of us in the body of Christ want to fulfill our personal pleasures or all of the things that my favorite person loves even if it causes you to compromise the standard of God. When we do this we are not positioned to win. You can't fulfill all righteousness by yourself.


Notice what Jesus said to John in verse 15 "for thus it becometh us to fulfill all righteousness". It took both of them to do it. The spiritual authority that God has placed over your life is designed to be a part of this with you. Who is with you? I would be a fool to think that I can accomplish the tremendous assignment of this ministry by myself. I need the help of the spiritual authority that is over me. I would also be a fool to think that everybody has to be just like me. Jesus said I have other sheep in *John 10:16 16 And other sheep I have, which are not of this fold: them also I must bring, and they shall hear my voice; and there shall be one fold, and one shepherd. KJV* This is confirmed in Luke when Jesus was talking to John about a person that was not with them. *Luke 9:49-50 And John answered and said, Master, we saw one casting out devils in thy name; and we forbad him, because he followeth not with us. And Jesus said unto him, Forbid him not: for he that is not against us is for us. KJV* Jesus told John to leave him alone. Jesus is not a groupie! Everybody will not be in your group. We have to let the people of God <u>be</u> the people of God and leave them alone. We have to be positioned to win. In addition, I need people who have the supply for the areas that I am weak in so that we all (the entire Church) can finish strong. We all have to make it across the finish line. If I make it across the finish line by myself, I did not win, I lost because we all have to make it.

I have to be able to stand up and say we won. Are we really committed to fulfill all righteousness? If not Satan knows that and when you we in the heat of the battle he calls you on it. I remember listening to great men and women of God and one of the things that they would always say when they were casting out demons is that Satan would rise up and say "I have a right to be here because they asked me to be here". When they would tell the demon to come out it would say no and the only way they could get that demon out is to get that person to repent and say that they don't want it any more. The Holy Spirit is the same way we have to ask Him to come in, He does not force His way in. Satan is devious when he gets us to participate in activities that invite him in. An example of those kinds of activities are office Christmas parties, happy hour etc., we may have to attend but we do not have to participate in what the king is eating.

(3) **Walk under an open heaven**. Do you realize that you could be sitting next to someone in church that is living under an open heaven and you are not? That is the reason that I like talking to people that I know are connected to God and are hearing Him because I need to know that the heaven is not closed over me.

*In Malachi 3:10 Bring ye all the tithes into the storehouse, that there may be meat in mine house, and prove me now herewith, saith the LORD of hosts, if I will not open you the windows of heaven , and pour you out a blessing, that there shall not be room enough to receive it. KJV* This is talking about the open heaven. Now if we are fulfilling all righteousness we don't have to talk about tithing because we are already being obedient to that. Since we are, heaven is open over us and, therefore, we are walking under an open heaven. If we don't tithe, heaven is closed and we do not hear what everybody is hearing. When you are in a battle, you have to have an open heaven because we need clear instructions about what we should do at this particular point. We need to know what God is saying. I received a call from someone that reminded me that I said that they could call me whenever they needed an answer to questions. She left the message that a lady on her job insisted that she let her take care of her dogs and lost one of them. She ended the call by requesting me to please call her back because felt like she wanted to go over to the lady's house and hurt her. Now she is using scripture to find her dog. That is what Saul did to find his father's donkey; he went to see the Prophet. Now, unfortunately, her emotions are way up and she needs to know what to do because if she acts on her emotions it will be the wrong thing. Many of us are listening to people who are under a closed heaven and we expect to win. Those that are doing that are not going to win because the people that they are listing to are not winning the battle. When you activate all four points you will win every battle. The final point is:

(4) **Receive the Spirit of God and walk in the light**. You have to walk in all the light that you know to walk in. Whatever revelation that you have received from the word of God do that is the light you know.

Remember the reason that I am talking about this is because God told me "I want you to prepare my people to exist on this battle ground" Remember that there is an external and an internal battle ground. The enemy never gets to your internal battle ground first, he comes into your external battle ground first in order to paralyze you and gain access to your internal which is your though realm. If he can paralyze you there he can shut you down.

The reason we think that he starts with our internal battle ground is because we look at it not from the perspective of being a battle ground, we look at it from the perspective of a manifestation. By way of manifestation he gets us to speak things that we would not ordinarily say. A famous person said this "if the enemy within cannot hurt you the enemy without can do you not harm". We give more attention to the enemy without and we are blind to the enemy within. The real enemy is in you. Say the word enemy very slowly—"En-e-my" if that can't hurt you, be confident that you will win every battle every time.

## Chapter 8

# Your Office Magnified

God woke me up one morning and I started to jot down some of the things he placed on my heart to share with this class. God said, I will *magnify your office*. He wasn't just talking to me. He was literally talking to the body of Christ. This is question number one. Do you know what your office is? If you have a challenge with understanding what that office is and the fact that you are standing in that office, you don't know what's being enlarged and being exposed. So you are being attacked in an area and you don't even know why. If God starts to *enlarge your office*, you must qualify for that office. Now a lot of us are kind of on the back side of the desert, there's nothing much happening and everything is pretty cool. The problem is, before you can enter into another level, before you enter into an office, you must qualify. So that's what we talk about to our students. If you are going to enter into the Office of a Prophet, you have to qualify for that office. The question is: are you qualified to stand in the Office of the Prophet? You may be in one of the other offices: Apostle, Evangelist, Pastor or Teacher, but the question remains, are you qualified for your office?

This gets really interesting to me. When God said "I will *magnify your office*" we have to understand exactly what that means. In other words, God is literally preparing you and me for something. I was being prepared in a time when I didn't realize I was being prepared. When I came into the knowledge of it, I had to cease to exist in my former manner. No matter what you need to do, you have to cease to exist as you did previously because you cannot function in an office as if you are not occupying the office. You just can't function that way.

There are a few things that I think we probably need to consider. First, we must understand that we have entered an unconditional agreement to the call. Your call is not conditional—it is unconditional, which means you can't back out of it. No matter what comes, no matter what the training, no matter what the pressure, no matter what happens in that office, you can't leave. Do we want this or not?

Do you realize that Jesus did not let everybody follow Him? There are conditions and they are found in Luke 14. The first time that I read this, I thought I was reading it wrong because I knew of a loving Jesus who loves everybody. There were people that He desired to follow Him but they made excuses and did not want to commit to the level that it took to follow Him. He said "You cannot be my disciple". That was amazing to me. I thought surely I must have missed some words or read the text incorrectly and needed to review it as I do on occasion.

Jesus tells this parable *Luke 14:16-26 16 Then said he unto him, A certain man made a great supper, and bade many: And sent his servant at supper time to say to them that were bidden, Come; for all things are now ready. And they all with one consent began to make excuse. The first said unto him, I have bought a piece of ground, and I must needs go and see it: I pray thee have me excused. And another said I have bought five yoke of oxen, and I go to prove them: I pray thee have me excused. And another said, I have married a wife, and therefore I cannot come. So that servant came, and shewed his lord these things.*

*Then the master of the house being angry said to his servant, Go out quickly into the streets and lanes of the city, and bring in hither the poor, and the maimed, and the halt, and the blind. And the servant said, Lord, it is done as thou hast commanded, and yet there is room. And the lord said unto the servant, Go out into the highways and hedges, and compel them to come in, that my house may be filled. For I say unto you, That none of those men which were bidden shall taste of my supper. And there went great multitudes with him: and he turned, and said unto them,* Notice what Jesus said in verse *If any man come to me, and hate not his father, and mother, and wife, and children, and brethren, and sisters, yea, and his own life also, he cannot be my disciple. KJV*

That word 'hate' in the Greek language means to love less. So if you don't love less, your mother, father, sister, brother and yourself also, you cannot be His disciple. On that information, how many of you would qualify as a disciple that will be able to follow Jesus? Do you realize that's a position that you have to grow to? Jesus hand-picked 12 people for the position and when they came into that position, they realized that there are no conditions on it. It is an unconditional position. I can't back out of this. I cannot '**not**' be on point.

Another principle I want to give you is that there is a testing moment for you as a prophet (or whatever office He is enlarging or magnifying). The question is: Can you make it through that testing period? Can you survive it?

One of the things that God spoke to me from the onset of this School of the Prophets is "The reason I want you to write your own material is because everybody else that's offering a program in your region are designing/executing it for individuals that are already prophets. It's curtailed for people that are already in that realm or vein". He said "I want you to do this from the material that I will give you and this is the reason. Another Touch of Glory, School of the Prophets works for anybody at any level because our assignment is to stop you from dying in the wilderness". Too many prophets die in the wilderness because they are not following anybody that has ever successfully made it through. That's a problem because we are constantly trying to follow somebody that just looks good. They have never, however, made it through anything, let alone a wilderness. So who are you following? How did they get to the place where they are? Did they opt to take a short cut and they haven't been through any tests? If they have not been through the test then they do not know the way out and they cannot go back and get someone else and bring them out.

I dare you to at least question those that say that they are Bishops. Who is it that consecrated you as Bishop? How did you get to be a Bishop and what was the process? Who consecrated you? If the answer is pastor so and so consecrated me, then you know that they skipped the process. There is an order and a process to become a Bishop, and that order requires at least three Bishops to consecrate one. There is a specific process that has to be completed. This is not a revelation that comes from heaven and all of a sudden God says to you, I'm calling you to be a Bishop. Bishops are not called. They are chosen.

Prophets, conversely, are called but just because God called you as a Prophet does not mean that you just go. There's a testing period. God calls you as an Apostle, Prophet, Evangelist, Pastor, or Teacher. A question is raised regarding even people who say that they are Prophets.

The question is who chose you? I question that. If you say that you are an Apostle, Prophet, Evangelist, Pastor, or Teacher and you are functioning in that office that God is going to enlarge or God is going to magnify, my number one question for you is, who chose you? They don't have to choose you as a Prophet because a Prophet is called, but then you have what we call the left hand of God, where all areas are chosen. Just like on the right hand of God you have Apostles, Prophets, Evangelists, Pastors and Teachers. The left hand matches the right hand and you have four fingers and a thumb as well, right. What do you have? You have the Bishop, Overseer, Elder, Deacon and Minister. All of those you had to be selected for and the left hand makes the right hand legal in the earth.

One of the reasons that your heavenly calling from heaven is no good in the earth is because you have not been chosen. Why, because nobody really knows you. Nobody has been able to follow you long enough to really be able to see here's an area where you have been perfected. You have already gone through the testing of a Prophet; you are pretty, pretty on point when it comes down to a prophetic declaration, who's challenging what you say? This is the reason that we are thoroughly against what we call back alley prophesy. Back alley prophesy is when the anointing was on the man or woman of God, they mis-heard God. This person then must grab you at the back of the church or in the parking lot and give you a prophesy that nobody can judge. Something is seriously wrong with that folks. You're caught when nobody else can hear what they said to you. It is absolutely out of order. Somebody that is watching over your soul should hear that word because they know you. They know your strengths and know where you are weak and what you are going through. They know whether or not you are ready to hear this. When you position yourself like that, you are in trouble.

God says I want to *magnify your office*; we need to make sure, then, that we have somebody in that office that has already been through some of these stages. What has happened in the body of Christ? We are Prophets and we want to put it on our cards. We got a word from heaven. Even worse, we have a word from prophet so and so that says we are prophets and we are already ready to do the work. No you are not. You've been to no school and you have no training.

Somebody said to me at one time, you talk about this School of the Prophet stuff; that's not in the Bible. I said it's not? I said, well you don't know your Bible then. There were Schools in Gilgal as recorded in II Kings the first and second chapters. There were a company of prophets that were there. The Senior Prophet was Elijah and the Budding Prophet was Elisha. We have the audacity to say that there are no prophets today and there are no Schools of the Prophets. No-- let me tell you why the School of the Prophets at one point, had to cease. God was no longer able to enlarge or magnify an office. He will not magnify a trashy office. You get magnified when you come out of the wilderness, not while you are in the wilderness. The office is never magnified in the wilderness. You have to come out. You have to prove that you can come out because when you come out, you have to be able to go back and get somebody.

In Joshua *3:7And the LORD said unto Joshua, This day will I begin to magnify thee in the sight of all Israel, that they may know that, as I was with Moses, so I will be with thee. KJV*

God had already spoken some things to Joshua. Joshua rose up early in the morning. He was raised from his place and came to this location where God could speak to him. So the purpose of magnifying the office is so that the people would know that as God was with whoever you were following, He will be with you. You see the problem now?

If we haven't been following anybody, we are self-made. You see how that messes up the pattern? When we don't have anyone over us, we have no covering. We, therefore have nothing for God to search and compare us with in regard to what He wants to continue to do. When you have not been searched and God wants to begin to *magnify your office*, what is He going to compare it to? "So as I was with Moses"—'as' is a comparative word. You need to look at what the 'as' is comparing that other thing to. "As I was with Moses, so I will be with Joshua". Look at your life, God is going to enlarge/*magnify your office*, right. How are you going to compare it? God will be with me as He was with my man or woman of God because we are not self-made. We were selected from a particular group.

I was sharing with someone this morning that my standards may be too high. Someone called me and wanted to know if I had somebody that I could send to carry Sunday and Wednesday services at their church. I began to think out of 27-30 leaders that we have, who can I send? I don't mind being open and transparent before you; I'm still thinking about who I can send. When I send them, they are going to represent me. So what I'm literally saying by sending them is "You are representing me and you will do it like I would do it".

Remember what Paul said regarding Timothy, "I have no one else". Wait a minute Paul, you raised up all of these churches, what do you mean you don't have anyone else to send? I have no one else outside of Timothy that will carry this out like I would carry it out. I'm enlarging the office. The question is: If God is magnifying the office, are those that are components of the office, being enlarged with the office? That is an enlargement of responsibility. In a position like that, who do you send? You mean to tell me you don't have anybody who is gifted enough? I have plenty of people who are gifted. You mean you don't have anybody that has an anointing on them? I have plenty of people who have an anointing on them. Then what are you looking for? Consistency!

It's going to take more than that you being gifted, anointed, and more than the fact that you have been through a storm and came out. Can we depend on you? That's the left hand of God. Can we depend on you? Are you going to get sick on me and have to call me on a Sunday morning? If you have a history of getting sick on a Sunday morning, I can't call you. Though you are anointed, though you are powerful and though you have all of this going for you, I can't call you because if you don't show up because you got sick, I look bad. I look at these factors, and I say who do I send? Who will go for me? I searched among them and I found none yet. There are some that I can send, but they have vital positions right here, and I cannot let them go on a Sunday. I cannot let them go on a Wednesday night because they are necessary to make what we do on a Wednesday work. Do we not have anyone? I'm talking to you. I'm trying to get you to question whether or not if you were in that position—are you able to be sent? Are you? Serious dilemma isn't it?

Consistency means that you are available to God. It has to be more than God knows me. God knows everything. God, however, put a man in charge of you so you would be able to say that 'as' God was with them, He will be with me. You have some measure of a pattern that can be clearly seen. God blessed them and He will bless me the same way He blessed them.

You have to enter an unconditional call. I have no conditions on my call. On Sunday mornings, whether I feel it or not, I've got to get up. It's not a feeling. People ask me sometimes, I

don't know how you keep going. What do you mean, how do
I do it? Well, don't you get tired? I don't think about whether
or not I'm tired. Don't you get frustrated? I don't think about
frustration. It's too big of a luxury for me to be able to afford.
I don't have time to get frustrated. I'm talking to prophets
today. I'm talking to you like this because when you step over
into this prophetic realm, you need to lose your will. You
don't have a will because God will have you to prophesy to
your enemies and you better mean it because you are the
mouth of God. God will have you to say something powerful
and positive to your enemy. What are you going to say?

Here's the question: Would that word that God has spoken to
you get hung up in the feelings that you are having over an
emotional area? Will they get hung up or will they flow freely
as God said? If it gets hung up in an emotional area, God
cannot enlarge that office. We don't have time to stand up and
use God's valuable time as a beating post. If they do, the
person is not ready. Why? They are using that which is
designed to position them to say something that is so
powerful, so amazing in people's lives. When one person
offended us, however, we then misuse them as a beating post.
We are going to beat everybody up because of one person's
offense. In the prophetic, you can't do that. You can't
prophesy on people what your wishes are because they
offended you. They have offended you, repented and gone on
about their business. It's all over. You, unfortunately, are still
caught up in the matter and you are the mouthpiece of God.
You need a bounce back anointing. That's when somebody
hits you and you have the opportunity to get offended, but you
bounce back.

Did you all get that? Not being offended at anyone. The word
offended or offend comes from a Greek word, which is scan
dal on. It's a scandal on you. That's the reason they offended

you and it looks like they are going on in Jesus because you are the one that the scandal is on. If you have a bounce back anointing, you can just bounce back from stuff quickly. You have six seconds to bounce back from an offense or it is going to begin to take root in your heart. That's anybody's heart.

Let me share something else regarding those six seconds. God has enabled me to totally transform my life and ministry with this principle. You need to know this if God is going to *enlarge your office*. Here it is. Between stimulus and response, there lies your power to choose. That means that I have six seconds in which I am totally in control. Most people don't utilize that six seconds, therefore, rather than becoming proactive, they are reactive. It effects everything that's going to happen in their future.

God is going to *enlarge your office* and people are going to recognize you for your office. The office that I am recognized in, at least across the United States, is in the area of the Prophet, and prophetic and leadership training. That's my dominant area. So that will be magnified. So within that six seconds—somebody does something that stimulates me to respond. Most people go ahead and respond. You smack me, I'm going to smack you back. That's it. This happens, that happens. You hurt me; I'm going to spend some money. It's across a wide plane. Let's look at that negative thing in your life. What is it that happened that caused you to respond that way? Between that thing that stimulated you and your responding, is the area that you are absolutely in control of and in this area I decide. I'm not responding to that because, when I do, that becomes my seed. In every seed lives a tremendous harvest. I don't want the results that it's going to bring. I would smack you back, but I don't want the harvest. How many of you got that? That's what we are missing in ministry. We are not in control. We have no discipline. That's what's missing in the area of the prophetic. I'm seeing prophets that have no discipline. Discipline must be built. It's not something that you are born with. If He is going to *magnify your office*, you are going to have to realize that you are in control after that thing has stimulated you. I'm in control of the six second's decision. I'm not going to be reactive, but proactive which means that I am in control of my decisions.

The other thing that it does, I had to battle through. When you deem that's how you are, you can blame no one for anything. Even if they made me mad, I can never ever use that again because that was only stimuli, wasn't it? The six seconds after that, I decide, I control, and I control my response. You are not in control my response. I am. So I can never blame you.

Let's shift as Prophets, and prophetic people into that realm because the word from God is He will *magnify your office*. I hope you grabbed every minute of what I've said because God is going to *magnify your office*.

You know what I want to deal with? I want to get you that are students out of this dimension of being wonderful in every area because you are not. There's an area in life where you dominate and you have to not mind saying so. It might be the area of finances, it may be the area of the prophetic, it may be the area of leadership, but find that area, because that's the office that God is going to magnify. That means that you will become an authority in that area.

One of the problems is that we are not an authority in any area. This is evident because when people look at you, they don't confuse you with what you do. They don't confuse your office with what you do. When people begin to think about the prophetic, the first person that comes to their mind ought to be you if that's the area that you are called to dominate.

Let me use myself as an example. I am sometimes tempted because I multi-task, to go outside of my area of domination and do this, that and the other. I absolutely love sales. I love to be able to put together a really strong marketing plan or business venture. The word that God spoke, however, was 'I will *magnify your office*'. I, therefore, have to consciously decide to not participate in some business ventures. I have to make myself not become dominant in that area because the area that you use your anointing in is going to minimize the area that you dominate. It's not the same area.

I want to send you out today with a challenge to think about what area you dominate. Now I'm talking to the students right here, but every one of us in this building dominate in a given area. Until we find that area, our names will never be confused with what we do. Never! I want my life to count. Don't you? You can make it count. How are you going to make it count? By maximizing your whole focus on the office that God told you to step into.

Let me close with this. He is going to *magnify your office*. So because He is going to *magnify your office*, you have to (1) know what office that is, and (2) what stream that office is designed to manifest for you.

For instance, if you stand in the Office of a Prophet, you have Market, Regional, Prophets to the Nations, Prophetic Dancers, Prophetic Writers, and the list goes on. We will talk about some of this in the next class. But which one of those streams do you dominate? Do you realize that a Market Place Prophet may be a prophet that never carries the title prophet because of where he's called to rule? You know how we violate them. We violate them by trying to snatch them into our church world and place a title on them. They don't want your title. They just want to do the assignment. They are Marketplace Prophets that will put your business, church, or ministry over the top if you just allow them to function. In addition, they prophesy in that realm better than the rest of us.

What area do you dominate? In the next class, I want to talk about areas of domination, magnifying your office in that area, etc. As a Prophet, it is my prayer that each class member discover which area they dominate.

There is an anointing that I want to release in this place today and I believe that God is going to shift each one of you so wonderfully into this next dimension as He magnifies your office.

Special Sessions

# Prophetic Dance, Praise and Worship

## The Prophetic Dancer

God has always wanted to communicate with earth. In fact, God came down in the cool of the day just to fellowship with Adam. Adam would talk with God and God with Adam. They would even walk together. In this day and time, God still desires to fellowship with us and to communicate with us in the earth. God wants to know what is going on in the earth and, in turn, he wants us to know what is going on in heaven. These things are often communicated by way of prophetic dances.

### The Dance of Victory

*And Miriam the prophetess, the sister of Aaron, took a timbrel in her hand; and all the women went out after her with timbrels and with dances. And Miriam answered them, Sing ye to the Lord, for he hath triumphed gloriously; the horse and his rider hath he thrown into the sea.*

*Exodus 15:20-21*

As we think upon this verse of scripture, we must visit the things that took place prior to this dance. In **Exodus 14:31** and in the beginning of **Exodus 15**, we see where Moses and the children of Israel began to sing unto the Lord. In other words, the prophetic song came forth as they were giving praises and exaltation unto God from their hearts. Following this, Miriam and the women came forth with the dance—the dance of victory.

Remember, as we discussed earlier concerning the prophetic, God is trying to communicate a message to earth. When earth receives this message, a response is required. Earth needs to respond to what heaven said. Whenever we operate in a victory dance, we won't always see the victory as a manifestation. What literally has to happen is that you must understand, as a prophetic dancer, what heaven has already proclaimed. Subsequently, if you dare to dance the dance of victory, victory *will* manifest.

In this account, we find that Miriam and all the women danced the dance of victory. What is so very interesting to note is how the author recognizes Miriam. The writer of Exodus recognizes her as *"Miriam the prophetess."* This specific recognition was made because it needed to be communicated that Miriam had a particular assignment.

This descriptive dance, which was given so that all of earth would know what heaven said, communicated something back to heaven. If we are really going to have manifestation in the earth, the dance needs to communicate something. All that we are doing as prophetic dancers is communicating something.

### The Dance of Rejoicing

*Hear the word of the Lord, O ye nations, and declare it in the isles afar off, and say, He that scattered Israel will gather him, and keep him as a shepherd doth his flock. For the Lord hath redeemed Jacob, and ransomed him from the hand of him that was stronger than he. Therefore they shall come and sing in the height of Zion, and shall flow together to the goodness of the Lord, for wheat, and for wine, and for oil, and for the young of the flock and of the herd: and their soul shall be as a watered garden; and they shall not sorrow any more at all. Then shall the virgin rejoice in the dance, both young men and old together: for I will turn their mourning into joy, and will comfort them, and make them rejoice from their sorrow.*     *Jeremiah 31:10-13*

Unlike the dance of victory, the dance of rejoicing does not communicate what heaven has said to earth, but it does the reverse. The dance of rejoicing communicates what earth is saying to heaven. With all that God is, he hates talking in the same way all of the time. Sometimes God might just say, "Dance before me." In other words, "Communicate something to me."

The sooner we realize that both verbal and non-verbal communication takes place between heaven and earth, the sooner we'll come to know that every time God does something, he looks for a response to begin in the earth. In this dance, earth is saying something to heaven that requires a response. How does God get this kind of communication between heaven and earth to take place? He places prophets and prophetic people in the earth.

If we were to teach this information to our prophetic dancers, our dancers wouldn't get up as if they were performing while dressed in scantily clothed and half-naked outfits. They would understand that God is actually watching and looking for the message—the message that's coming from the prophetic dancers. Prophetic dancers are to communicate something that is prophetic, not pathetic.

## The Dance of Praise

*Praise ye the Lord. Sing unto the Lord a new song, and his praise in the congregation of saints. Let Israel rejoice in him that made him: let the children of Zion be joyful in their King. Let them praise his name in the dance: let them sing praises unto him with the timbrel and harp.*

According to **Psalm 8:2**, praise stills the Enemy and the avenger. The Enemy cannot move when praise is going on, regardless of the type of praise that is offered.

It is through praise that God stills or stops the Enemy and the avenger. Praise itself is in the earth. It is a communication to God. Praise stirs God up, but it is simply a communication. Yet when God hears praise, what he actually hears is a reason to recognize earth. God sees the agony, the trials, and the tribulations of the people. When praise is coming from agony, trials, or tribulations, the sound is different. This kind of praise has a different sound, such as the kind of praise David offered as a sacrifice.

## The Dance of Sacrifice

*And it was told king David, saying, The Lord hath blessed the house of Obed-edom, and all that pertaineth unto him, because of the ark of God. So David went and brought up the ark of God from the house of Obed-edom into the city of David with gladness. And it was so, that when they that bare the ark of the Lord had gone six paces, he sacrificed oxen and fatlings. And David danced before the Lord with all his might; and David was girded with a linen ephod. So David and all the house of Israel brought up the ark of the Lord with shouting, and with the sound of the trumpet. And as the ark of the Lord came into the city of David, Michal Saul's daughter looked through a window, and saw King David leaping and dancing before the Lord; and she despised him in her heart.* 2 *Samuel 6:12-16*

David danced with all of his might. In this, he offered a sacrifice unto the Lord. If you are dancing through a sacrifice, a tribulation, or an agonizing experience, the sound of that praise is different. It is similar to the cry to a mother from her child who wants to get his brother in trouble although the brother is not really bothering him. That kind of cry is different from the cry that comes forth when that brother is trying to kill him. It is a different sound.

The one who is designed to hear and interpret the sound knows which sound is which. God is the one who is designed to hear our praise, and he realizes what our praises are born of. So, when the prophetic dancers are dancing the dance of praise, God looks to determine what the praise is actually coming from.

Verses 13 and 14 tell us, *"...when they that bare the ark of the Lord had gone six paces, he sacrificed oxen and fatlings. And David danced before the Lord with all his might; and David was girded with a linen ephod."* What it does not tell us in such plain terms is that David also sacrificed. David offered a sacrifice by dancing with all of his might. He gave all that he had in the dance. This communicated something to God, and God recognized this.

In verses 13-15, it is apparent that there is an order. The shouting in verse 15 did not take place until there was an end of sacrificing. The oxen were sacrificed, the fatlings were sacrificed, David was sacrificed, and afterwards the shouting or praise was given. Certainly, let things be done decently and in order.

## The Dance of Response

*Verily I say unto you, Among them that are born of women there hath not risen a greater than John the Baptist: notwithstanding he that is least in the kingdom of heaven is greater than he. And from the days of John the Baptist until now the kingdom of heaven suffereth violence, and the violent take it by force. For all the prophets and the law prophesied until John. And if ye will receive it, this is Elias, which was for to come. He that hath ears to hear, let him hear. But whereunto shall I liken this generation? It is like unto children sitting in the markets, and calling unto their fellows, And saying, We have piped unto you, and ye have not danced; we have mourned unto you, and ye have not lamented.*               *Matthew 11:11-17*

There is a generation that is both hard of hearing and insensitive to the Spirit of God. In this season when we are so hard of hearing, God raises up prophetic dancers to communicate to a body of people exactly what he is saying because dancers command our attention. We must train the dancers!

*And saying, We have piped unto you, and ye have not danced; we have mourned unto you, and ye have not lamented.*            *Matthew 11:17*

In this verse, heaven essentially said that a sound went out to the people, but they either did not hear the sound or refused to dance when they heard it. The real purpose of the prophetic dancer is to communicate a message.

The message could be one of warfare, healing, or deliverance. The prophetic dancer, like singers, set the atmosphere for the word of God to come forth. While they dance, heaven listens for the message. Keep in mind that earth only dances according to the sound heard from heaven.

As prophetic dancers, prophets, and prophetic people we must come to the realization that nothing originates in the earth. Everything comes from heaven, even the very things we pray for. We simply respond to what heaven desires, whether it be in dance, instruments, or prophecy.

## The Prophetic Psalmist

One of the things that are imperative that we embrace is the idea of different methods of expression. God deals with us in various ways; he deals with the entire body of Christ.

As God begins to bring the prophetic to its peak, it's going to be absolutely necessary that we understand all of the different components of the prophetic and all of the different ways in which God is trying to send a signal to the body of Christ.

We must take hold of the fact, as it pertains to the prophetic, that God is trying to say something. One of the amazing things about God is that He will go through any means necessary to get a message to His people. It's not like God just says something one time and then says, "Okay, forget it! They didn't hear me when I said what I said. Now, I'm just going to go ahead and do this." God never says that unless we are so mature in Him that He expects that we hear Him the first time that He speaks.

God deals with us at various levels. In these different levels, it is important for us to understand that God views everyone at their different levels and bases an individual's level on how many ways He's going to try to get His message to them. If we are mature in God, the methods that He will use to get the message to us will be very limited. On the other hand, if we are immature in God, He will go to any extreme to ensure we receive His message. Keep in mind, though, that all of us are limited in at least two areas. We are limited in our understanding, and we are limited according to the dispensation in which we live. Yet, it bears repeating that God will go to extremes to get His message to His people.

Through and by this lesson, we will see how powerful the prophetic psalmist is. The assignment of the *Prophetic Psalmist* is to operate in poetry and yet communicate a message prophetically. Basically, this is what happens in a lot of our songs. A message was communicated. A message was communicated that was going to deal greatly with something that was to come.

*My God, my God, why hast thou forsaken me? Why art thou so far from helping me, and from the words of my roaring? O my God, I cry in the daytime, but thou hearest not; and in the night season, and am not silent. But thou art holy, O thou that inhabitest the praises of Israel. Our fathers trusted in thee: they trusted, and thou didst deliver them. Psalm 22: 1-4*

*They cried unto thee, and were delivered: they trusted in thee, and were not confounded. But I am a worm, and no man; a reproach of men, and despised of the people. All they that see me laugh me to scorn: they shoot out the lip, they shake the head, saying. He trusted on the Lord that he would deliver him: let him deliver him, seeing he delighted in him. But thou art he that took me out of the womb: thou didst make me hope when I was upon my mother's breasts. I was cast upon thee from the womb: thou art my God from my mother's belly. Be not far from me; for trouble is near; for there is none to help. Many bulls have compassed me: strong bulls of Bashan have beset me round. They gaped upon me with their mouths, as a ravening and a roaring lion. I am poured out like water, and all my bones are out of joint: my heart is like wax; it is melted in the midst of my bowels. My strength is dried up like a potsherd; and my tongue cleaveth to my jaws; and thou hast brought me into the dust of death.*

*Psalm 22:5-15*

As we begin to talk about this prophet type, please consider how far in advance this psalm was actually given to David. Isn't it exciting to know that God is still delivering messages in this manner? Especially if we're operating as prophetic psalmists and not just trying to package a bunch of poems that we can sell. The intended purpose for the prophetic psalmist's assignment is to make sure that a message from God was sent, not to sell poems, even though these kinds of prophetic messages have been marketed and sold in the marketplace.

We must keep in mind, though, that the original intent was to make sure that God got a message out that may or may not have been recognized as a message of God. Eventually this message found its way into the right hands and communicated to the people exactly what God wanted to communicate. We cannot take the prophetic psalmists or their assignment for granted. Some people have this gift, but the prophetic psalmists don't turn on until they begin to write. As long as they try to give a message in tongues or attempt to give a verbal prophetic message, the gift lies dormant and never turns on. It only turns on when they begin to write. It is when the prophetic psalmist begins to write that the prophetic turns on and revelation comes from God as it pertains to what God wants the earth to know.

By now, it's not difficult to determine that this prophetic message found in Psalms 22 is dealing with Jesus' crucifixion. Take notice that this prophetic message relays, almost word for word, what took place on the cross even though the message was written thousands of years before the crucifixion.

What God was actually doing thousands of years prior was giving David poetry regarding something that was going to take place on the cross. Amazing! To see that God could deal with a prophetic poet, give this poet a particular message, inscribe this message, and walk out the message—almost word for word—on the cross is nothing short of amazing! Even greater than that is the fact that sinners who had no clue at all regarding the Word of God were able to see and read what this prophetic psalmist wrote about what would take place on the cross.

*"He trusted on the Lord that he would deliver him: let him deliver him, seeing he delighted in him."* Psalm 22:8 is one of the actual statements made at the Calvary scene. It was even spoken by people who couldn't recall what David said. They may have even been unaware of the writings of David.

Verse 14, *"I am poured out like water, and all my bones are out of joint: my heart is like wax; it is melted in the midst of my bowels,"* depicts another portion of the scene at Calvary. Some of what David has written is very descriptive of what took place on the cross. You'll never be able to find this in the book of Matthew. Only God, thousands of years prior, could actually illustrate to us what was taking place on the inside of the body of Jesus as he was beaten and hung from the cross. No one who was present at the crucifixion described what occurred inside of the body of Jesus. David, the prophetic psalmist gave us an X-ray vision version of what happened at the cross.

Don't, however, become so engrossed with these details that you forget who communicated this information. The individual who actually communicated this message was a prophetic psalmist. It must be understood that what this prophet received was revelation that was coming to him after he began to write. Please know that this doesn't just turn on when you understand that you are writing prophetically. This turns on whenever you take hold of the pen. Your writing tool of choice becomes an instrument that activates what is on the inside of you. Anytime you get your pen, it starts to turn on.

Because we've been so spiritually minded, we thought that in order for it to turn on, we had to be dealing with a biblical subject. In reality, it doesn't matter if it's a biblical subject or not. You could write about anything that God wants to talk to you about. There is not a subject in the earth that God doesn't know about. God is omniscient. He knows everything.

If we fully understood this concept, books would come out of us once we applied pen to paper. A lot of times you may start off the work. But, you have to be sensitive enough to the Holy Ghost to know when he turned on. Not everything that you write, obviously, is God. Just because you are a prophet and may even be a prophetic psalmist, not everything you write is of God. Therefore, you must be sensitive to know when the Holy Ghost starts and when he ends. All that remains needs to be edited out if we are really going to term our work as "prophetic poetry."

A very chill-provoking statement representing Jesus' statement, "I thirst," is found in the fifteenth verse: "*My strength is dried up like a potsherd; an my tongue cleaveth to*

*my jaws; and thou hast brought me into the dust of death. "*
The word "potsherd" is likened to sun-baked clay. If you
know anything about sun-baked clay, you know that it is dry,
cracked, and so devoid of any moisture that you can actually
take it in your hands and break it. When Jesus declared, "I
thirst," that is what the inside of his mouth was like. It was so
dry that his tongue literally stuck to the roof of his mouth.
How he managed, in this parched condition, to say, "It is
finished," is beyond me. Yet, thousands of years prior to
Jesus' crucifixion, God gave poetry to a man named David.
And, through the writing of his poetry, David intimately
depicted the details of an incident that would not take place
until years and years following his writing. The psalmist,
David, had no clue regarding what he wrote about; but at the
same time, he knew that he was to write this psalm. In his
writing, he was actually unfolding the scene and events of the
cross.

If we are going to understand the power of being a prophetic
psalmist, we need to understand that every time we pick up a
pen and a piece of paper, God unfolds the future to us through
this prophet type.

# Order Form

## Bishop R S Walker Ministries

2760 Crain Highway
Waldorf, MD 20601
301- 843-9267 • Fax 240-585-7093
www.bishoprswalkerproducts.com
email: admin@bishoprswalker.com

**Items Ordered:**

Name
_____

Title                                    Date
_____

Church/Ministry
_____

Address
_____

City                          State           Zip
_____

Daytime Phone                      Email
_____

**Items Ordered:**

| Description | CD | DVD | Qty | Total |
|---|---|---|---|---|
| Raising Prophets of Character Book | | | | $14.95 |
| School of the Prophets 15-week Course | | $190.00 | Discount | $110.00 |
| School of the Prophets Live Training | | | | $250.00 |
| School of Prophetic Intercession | | | | $200.00 |
| Prophetic Dominion Series | $34.00 | $47.00 | | |
| Renaissance Prophet's Manual | | | | $33.95 |
| The Art of Tongues Book | | | | $ 9.99 |
| Raising Prophets Prayer Devotional | | | | $14.99 |
| Creating Habits for a Functional Life | | | | $14.99 |
| The Father Son Encounter | | | | $16.95 |
| The Fundamentals of Faith (6-CDs) | $50 | | | |
| The Power of First Fruit Offering (6-CDs) | $30 | $60 | | |

**Shipping Information:**
Add $5 for Priority Mail first item
$1 per additional item
MD add 6% sales tax

| | |
|---|---|
| Total price of items | |
| Add shipping charge | |
| Tax (if applicable) | |

**Method of Payment:**

Please charge my:   □ Discover  □ MasterCard  □ VISA  □ AMEX

Card Number: ☐☐☐☐☐☐☐☐☐☐☐☐☐☐

Exp Date (Month/Year): ☐☐ / ☐☐

Signature (as shown on credit card): _____

☐ Check or Money Order

**For Speaking Engagements contact:**
Office of Bishop Administrative Staff
Ph:  (301) 843-9267/(877) 200-8967
Fx:  (240) 585-7093

*9 7 8 0 6 9 2 4 3 4 6 5 9*